"It's Just What I've Always Wanted!"

A STONESONG PRESS BOOK

HYPERION   NEW YORK

More than 2,000
Imaginative and Unique
Gifts—from a Ride in a MiG
Jet to a Singing Telegram

Chiquita Woodard

Copyright © 1998 The Stonesong Press, Inc., and Chiquita Woodard

Library of Congress Cataloging-in-Publication Data
Woodard, Chiquita
    "It's just what I've always wanted!" : more than 2,000 imaginative and unique gifts—from a ride in a MiG jet to a singing telegram / Chiquita Woodard.
       p.   cm.
    "A Stonesong Press Book."
    Includes index.
    ISBN 0-7868-8330-8
    1. Gifts—Directories.   I. Title.
GT3040.W66   1998
394—dc21   98–17029
                                            CIP

Designed by Lovedog Studio

First Edition

10 9 8 7 6 5 4 3 2 1

For Bo and the boys:
Revel, Spencer, and Simon

Acknowledgments

I am grateful to all of my friends who have encouraged me and offered their great ideas, especially Susan Berthiaume, Kathryn Black, Gaylen Blankenship, Frish Brandt, George and Susan Clark, Marshall Crossman, Mercedes Feller, Susan Goldthwaite, Lucy Hilmer, Leslie Leslie, Joan O'Conner, my sister, Jan Kolb, and Kate Gruen, the world's best neighbor. Special thanks to Alison Fargis Beran at The Stonesong Press, and to my editor, Laurie Abkemeier.

Contents

7 Rites of Passage and Personal Achievements 120

8 Feel Better   134

9 Special Days   144

10 On the Job   157

"It's Just What I've Always Wanted!"

Introduction

Everyone loves gifts. In our society, gifts are given to recognize birthdays, anniversaries, religious celebrations, and rites of passage. Sometimes we give gifts to say "thank you," or "feel better," and sometimes we give them for no reason at all. Gifts are offered to mark the beginning of life, the end of life, and all the important events in between. We give gifts to bind relationships and to let people know we are thinking of them.

For many people, choosing a gift can be an anxiety-ridden experience. Not everyone loves to shop, but we all need to buy gifts several times each year. It's difficult to find time to take care of the basics these days, and shopping is no longer a recreational activity, so we don't have a lot of time to look. And, although we want to give a wonderful gift, we don't always know what will please. With this book, you will be able to find the perfect gift for everyone, and for every occasion. It is filled with over two thousand gift ideas and divided by specific gift-giving occasions. I encourage you to read it cover to cover, because you may find the perfect Father's Day gift in the "On the Job" chapter (a **leather mouse pad**, perhaps), or the perfect present for your sister's wedding in "I Love You!" (maybe a **stack of romantic CDs** or a **volume of**

romantic poetry). In addition, an appendix lists gifts by category, including Sports Fan, the Gourmet, and the Discerning Teen.

As America Online's Gift Expert, I gave advice to thousands of people looking for that special gift. And as a professional buyer for the past fifteen years, I have traveled the globe, always on the lookout for treasures. I have shopped in hundreds of stores and perused every catalog imaginable in my search for what I consider to be the best. I have also turned to friends, who have generously shared with me their best gift ideas. I have included gifts in a wide range of prices for all types and ages of people. Since we have so little time these days, the emphasis is on purchased gifts rather than homemade ones, but you will also find thoughtful ideas not found in any store. Prices, where mentioned, were correct at the time of this writing, but should be considered approximate, and used as guidelines only. Hundreds of sources are included in Appendix B.

The variety of gifts is infinite. The perfect gift can be wildly extravagant, like a **silk and cashmere robe**, or a **ride in a MiG jet**, or it can cost nothing, like writing a **love letter**. It can be an object, an idea, or a gesture. Although more than a thousand suggestions for all of these appear throughout this book, the ideas contained here are not meant to be exhaustive. As much as anything, this book is intended to stimulate creativity. As you browse through the chapters, let your imagination wander and see what ideas come to mind.

The more personalized your gift is, the more meaningful it will be. Perhaps the most personal gift you can give is your time or talent, and the recipient of such a gift will feel truly flattered. Assess your skills: What do you have or know how to do that others want? A talent you take for granted may be prized by someone else if you're willing to give it away.

Gift-giving is an act of kindness for the giver and the receiver. It should not be approached as a competition to see who can spend the most money. The presentation and the thoughtful note that accompany it are at least as important as the gift itself. You'll find a lot of helpful ideas about gift wrapping and cards in the last chapter, "Wrap It Up."

Gift giving doesn't have to be time-consuming or anxiety provoking. In fact, it can be very satisfying if you follow a few guidelines.

Get Organized!

Like so many things in life, gift shopping is a lot more successful if you don't wait until the last minute. You'll enjoy yourself more, find more suitable gifts, and probably stick to a budget more easily if you plan ahead. Timeliness is essential to the art of gift giving. No matter how old we get, a birthday is a special day for the person celebrating it. A belated birthday greeting or gift just isn't the same; a day later, or a week later is no longer a special day, and the impact of your greeting or gift will be diminished.

Not only can gift-giving be fun and effortless, it can be an expression of your own creativity. Start by putting yourself in the place of the person you're buying for. What do you know about that person? What do they care about—fitness, books, education, art, business, the environment, food, themselves?

If your gift requires that you go shopping, have a few clear ideas in mind; otherwise, it can be overwhelming. You may find it's more fun and productive to team up with a friend who loves to shop and has great taste.

Keep a remembrance calendar of special days. (The Metropolitan Museum of Art, 800-468-7386, usually features one in their catalog for under $10, as do the Papyrus stores across the country.) It's important that it be perpetual, so you don't have to fill it out every year. Hang the calendar on your wall, right next to your desk, or wherever you know you'll see it regularly. Or use Appendix C to keep track.

Include all of the important dates in your life: birthdays of your partner, children, grandchildren, siblings, parents, in-laws, friends, friends' children, associates, and pets; anniversaries, Valentine's Day, Christmas, Hanukkah, Kwanzaa, Mother's Day, Father's Day, Grandparents Day. Your calendar could also include Easter, Halloween, the solstices and equinoxes, Saint Patrick's Day, Secretary's Day—if these are holidays you celebrate. Get in the habit of referring to your calendar frequently and adding to it often. This is not the place to write down business meetings or dental appointments; it should be devoted exclusively to celebrating others.

You'll enjoy the time you spend sending cards and writing notes to people acknowledging their special days. Take a few minutes every week or so, sit back with your calendar and some beautiful stationery, and express your thoughtfulness.

This remembrance calendar itself makes a great gift for someone you are close to, especially if it is given with a few important dates noted personally by you. You can collect these dates easily by passing the calendar around at a holiday dinner or some other family gathering, and asking people to enter their birthdays, anniversaries, and other special occasions.

If you're more technically oriented, you may already have the Claris Organizer or similar software for your computer. These programs allow you to keep track of special occasions with ease. For example, Claris Organizer not only will color-code by category, it will give you reminders in advance, and repeat annually, if you wish.

To accompany your computer organizer or Special Days Calendar, keep an accordion file, divided and labeled according to occasion and filled with cards for every contingency: birthday, new baby, get well, anniversary, and blank cards (my favorite because they'll work for everything).

If you aspire to become an exceptional gift giver, keep a selection of gift-wrapping paper and greeting cards handy (see Chapter 12, "Wrap It Up"), as well as a cache of potential presents, for those times when you're caught off-guard. Take advantage of seasonal sales to stockpile gifts for the events that occur often in your life. If your child attends a lot of birthday parties, you might have handy several book titles to appeal to her age group. If you're invited to dinner frequently, have a selection of specialty foods, wine, or champagne readily available, and silk or brocade bags to wrap them in. Pins, pens, and scarves are useful to have around for teachers' gifts. Of course, it's nicer to shop individually for gifts, with the recipient's tastes and interests in mind, but that's not always possible, so having a supply of all-purpose gifts ready to wrap will keep you from panicking.

Gift-Giving Hints

1. Be simple. Sometimes the classics work best, and one small gift can convey the most heartfelt sentiment.

2. Be extravagant. If the person likes bubble gum, give them five hundred pieces. Fill the room with fifty helium balloons. If she wears ribbons in her hair, buy them for her in every color of the rainbow. If he's nuts about Ovaltine, give him a whole case of it. Being extravagant does not have to mean spending a lot; rather it is a reflection of a generous spirit.

3. It is said that you should not give artwork as a gift, because the choice is too personal, but some of my favorite pieces of art are those given to me by a photographer or painter. It is a highly personal gift, a piece of the artists themselves, and that is why it means so much to me.

4. When you're traveling, keep your eyes open for little items particular to the region that will be special back home: bagels from New York City, maple syrup from Vermont, a Cajun sauce from New Orleans, a chile ristra from Santa Fe, an Eiffel Tower keychain from Paris. When I'm in England I always buy a supply of Maldon's Sea Salt to give to friends, because even though it is in every grocery store in England, you can't find it in the United States. Even ubiquitous tourist souvenirs can be novel out of context.

5. Above all, put your heart into it—if you can do this well, you will come up with the perfect gift.

1

Happy Birthday

The best thing about birthdays is that they give us a chance to focus all of our attention on a single person for a whole day. This opens up a lot of creative possibilities, so be imaginative, and have fun with it. Plan an outing. Spoil the birthday boy or girl. Make a dream come true. Phone if you can't make a personal appearance. But whatever you do, make sure the birthday person feels truly celebrated and ready to take on whatever the next year brings.

Happy Birthday to You

One of my favorite things to do for a friend's birthday is to **call him or her up and sing "Happy Birthday."** You can do it by yourself or get friends and family to join in. Either way, it's fun for everyone on both ends of the phone.

Musical birthday greetings for people of all ages can also be delivered by calling SEND-A-SONG (800-736-3276). For about $9.95, they'll call on the date and time you request, and play your personal message, along with a song you can choose from their extensive list.

How about the Beatles' "Birthday," or Altered Images' "Happy Birthday"? For a more romantic birthday message, try "Sixteen Candles."

For a nostalgic musical touch, give the birthday celebrant a tiny **hurdy-gurdy** that cranks out strains of "Happy Birthday." At $2.75, you can afford to buy a handful of them, and attach one to every birthday gift you give (Dandelion, 888-548-1968).

Take the Cake

The best birthday cakes are homemade, and taking the time to bake one is a great gift in itself. If it's just a little off kilter or the frosting sags a bit, so much the better. But many of the recipes are just beyond me—way too complicated! This one will never let you down—it looks beautiful, has a fine, light crumb, and tastes terrific. Success is assured, even for the first-time cake baker. (Note: Don't feel you must save it just for birthdays; any occasion is given more stature when it is celebrated with a cake.)

Kate's Cake

*2 tablespoons vegetable shortening and 2 tablespoons flour, for
  greasing and dusting pans
1 cup milk, at room temperature
¾ cup egg whites (5 or 6) at room temperature
2 teaspoons almond extract
1 teaspoon vanilla extract
2¼ cups cake flour
1¾ cups sugar
4 teaspoons baking powder
1 teaspoon salt
12 tablespoons unsalted butter, softened*

Preheat oven to 350°. Use shortening and flour to coat two 9-inch round pans. Pour milk, egg whites, and extracts into a 2-cup glass measure, mix with a fork until blended. Mix flour, sugar, baking powder, and salt in the bowl of an electric mixer, at slow speed. Add butter and continue to beat until mixture resembles crumbs, with no powdery ingredients remaining. Add all but ½ cup of the milk mixture. Beat at medium speed for 1½ minutes. Add remaining ½ cup of milk mixture and beat 30 seconds more. Scrape bowl, and beat 20 seconds more. Pour into prepared cake pans. Bake 23 to 25 minutes. Allow to rest 3 minutes before removing from pans. When thoroughly cooled, spread with:

Foolproof Fudge Frosting

12 ounces bittersweet chocolate (the best you can find)
1²/₃ cups heavy cream (not ultra-pasteurized)
2 teaspoons vanilla or 2 tablespoons cognac
¼ cup unsalted butter, softened

Break chocolate into pieces and whirl in food processor until very fine. Heat cream to boiling and add to chocolate; pour through feeder tube with the motor running. Process a few seconds until smooth. Stir in vanilla or cognac, add butter, and mix briefly. Allow to cool to spreading consistency.

If you just don't have time to bake, you can always rely on your local bakery. Or, if the birthday is happening on the other side of the country, you can **send a cake** from Piece of Cake (800-922-5390). Another thought for someone who lives elsewhere, hates cake, or is watching her weight, is the **Birthday Flower Cake** ($39.99) from 800-FLOW-ERS. It looks just like a cake, comes in a bakery box, complete with real candles, but is actually an arrangement of flowers that lasts for a week.

Chocolate fans will love the **Happy Birthday in a Box**, which contains balloons and five candles that fit on the "cake," actually a one-pound bar of chocolate. A ready-made party! ($18, next-day delivery available, 911 Gifts, on-line at www.911gifts.com)

Don't settle for just any old birthday candles if you're in charge of the cake. For an elegant look, you can get ultra-thin, 8-inch-long tapers in five assorted colors ($9.95, Illuminations, 800-CANDLES). Tie a big bundle of them onto a special birthday package. The can't-blow-out candles are fun—keep a supply on hand to lend a little sparkle to those sometimes dull birthday dos at the office.

Just for Kids

Birthdays are special occasions throughout our lives, but never more so than in childhood. We look forward not only to gathering in celebration with friends, but also to getting one year older, and gaining the maturity and privileges that go with it. As adults, each year is much like the next, and the distinctions diminish, but to a child, one year makes a world of difference.

Of course, birthdays are special because children love to receive presents, but often, those "must-have" toys are quickly discarded. If you're shopping for your own child, a grandchild, or a friend's child, try to remember what you or your children loved, and trust that instinct. The tried-and-true gifts tend to have more lasting value than the latest fad. Some of the very best gifts for younger ones, or kids of any age, are homemade creations. These include **tire swings**, **rope swings**, and **seesaws**.

At the time of a child's first birthday, you can begin a **Birthday Yearbook**, which can be updated annually. Start with a blank book; you may want to put a facsimile of the birth certificate, a newborn photo, or some original artwork on the cover. At each birthday attach a current photograph of him, along with your personal recollections, and ask guests or family members to write a few thoughts about your child in the book. These jottings could be physical descriptions, memories, or musings on his personality. Photographs of the celebration can also be included. Imagine how much fun it will be for him to see his old birthday photos and read the book as he grows.

When your child is a toddler, you can make her a **Circle of Friends tablecloth**, embroidering her name and birth date in the center of a large piece of washable cotton muslin. Each year at her birthday celebration friends and family are invited to trace their handprints onto the tablecloth with colorful markers. Artwork should be encouraged as well, and as the years pass the birthday girl will be reminded of all of the friends who have gathered to help celebrate her.

One friend celebrates her daughter's birthday each year by giving her a treasure from her own childhood. Through the years, the gifts have included a rocking horse, a near life-size stuffed leopard, a child's chair, her collection of Ginny dolls, and a bicycle she constructed out of spare parts, to look just like the old clunker she rode as a kid. She has photographs of herself as a young girl—holding the doll, riding the bike, and so forth—and she passes on the photographs with the gifts. If you haven't saved possessions from long ago, you can look for modern substitutes. The same friend receives from her father every year a little piece of her past childhood: one year it was the girl-child from her dollhouse family; another year, silver salt and pepper shakers that had been a gift from her father to her mother; and later, her deceased mother's wedding ring. These gifts trigger memories that mean much more to her than anything her father could buy.

Another option is a **cookie cutter handprint**. Send a tracing of the child's hand, and three to four weeks later you'll receive the cutter. Made of heavy-gauge aluminum, it comes engraved with the child's name, age, and a message of up to six words. This can be an annual gift, resulting in a very personal, graduated set of hands. Available for $15 from Cookie Cutters by Karen, 888-476-4525.

One of my favorite gifts for wee ones is a **little chair**—every child should have one. This can be given as a gift at birth, to grow into, or to someone who is at the learning-to-walk stage. The child can push the chair around for stability, and later, use it to reach high places like light switches or the bathroom sink. My oldest son's "brown chair," a gift from an antiques dealer friend when Revel was little, is now as revered among the family antiques as great-grandmother's walnut armoire. There are a lot of chairs to choose from, old and new, Adirondacks, rockers, cleverly painted pricey ones, and inexpensive garage sale or flea market models. L.L. Bean (800-221-4221) has a **Child's Keepsake Rocker** ($69)—available in red, blue, green, or natural—which you can have personalized.

For a one-year-old, some of the classics include a **popcorn popper push toy**, **wooden pegs and hammer toy**, and **cloth or cardboard books**. Dandelion (888-848-1968) has nesting and stacking **ABC blocks** with an old world look (set of ten, $18).

As the child grows a little older, **gardening tools**, a **red wagon full of wooden blocks**, a **toddler gym**, or a **peddle car** are good

Gifts for the Gardener

* **Japanese Okubo shears**, $27, touted as her all-time favorite gift by Alta Tingle, owner of my all-time favorite store, The Gardener, in Berkeley (510-548-4545).
* **Bulldog Tools of England**, the finest gardening tools in the world, and the ones that put Smith & Hawken on the map, are now available only from Seeds of Change, 888-762-7333 (**spade and fork**, $49 each; **hand fork and trowel**, $15 each).
* **A kneeler stool** ($30, Brookstone, 800-351-7222).
* **Swiss Felco pruners** ($50 from Seeds of Change, 888-762-7333).
* **A manicure**—it won't last for long, but it'll be a treat while it does.
* *Classic Roses* by Peter Beales—the definitive rose lover's guide ($55, Henry Holt & Co.).
* **Gloves** from Womanswork (800-536-2305).
* **A garden tour of England** ($4,000–5,000, Smith & Hawken, 888-524-3573, or call your travel agent).
* **A subscription** to *Garden Design* (800-234-5118) or the luscious British magazine, *Gardens Illustrated*.
* **A collection of antique roses** (Heirloom Garden Roses, 503-538-1576).
* **A little box of rock candy** (Any gardener will understand! $10.50 at Dandelion, (888-548-1968).
* **Several packets of heirloom vegetable seeds** (Seeds of Change, 888-762-7333).

* **A handblown glass hyacinth forcing jar** ($10–20, The Gardener, 510-548-4545).
* **Daffodil bulbs for naturalizing** (White Flower Farm, 800-503-9624).
* **Half a dozen paperwhite bulbs**, shipped at two-week intervals from October through February, to take the edge off winter. Send along a supply of pebbles the color of robin's eggs, or black polished Japanese river stones, to plant them in (The Gardener, 510-548-4545).
* **A pair of kitschy pink flamingos** for the lawn ($19.95, The Mind's Eye, 800-949-3333).
* **A sterling silver watering can key ring** ($95, Tiffany's, 800-526-0649).
* **A collection of culinary herbs** including sage, marjoram, and purple oregano, tied with a raffia bow ($39, 800-FLOWERS).
* **Potted herbs**, ready for garden planting or windowsill growing (choose from two hundred varieties, $2.50–4.00 on-line at Garden Escape, www.garden.com).
* **A collection of scented geraniums**—choose from over thirty scents including coconut, rose, lemon, cinnamon, and one that smells just like fresh doughnuts! ($24, Logee's Greenhouses, 888-330-8038).

Man's Best Friend

* Visit the web site of Aardvark Pets (www.aardvarkpet.com), an on-line store dedicated to pets and people who love them. Their biggest hit? **Virtual Catz and Dogz**, for people who want the fun of owning a pet without all the hassle and responsibility of an actual physical being. These on-line animals do tricks on the computer screen. This is also the place to buy doggie apparel: **tee-shirts of all your favorite college and NFL teams**—in a variety of sizes to fit all the canine boosters on your list—as well as **pet pearls, a gold lame bow tie**, and, yes, even **hiking boots! Bark Bars**, shaped like cats and postmen, are available in a two-pound tin for $17. Of course, they also have all the normal stuff, like **collars**, **leashes**, and **bowls**.

* A **giant, refillable Milk-Bone tin**, chock full of what else? ($14, Dandelion, 888-548-2968).

* Ask your butcher for knuckle bones—they're usually happy to give them to you free of charge.

* Make **a doggie birthday cake**: a mound of cooked ground lamb, "frosted" with creamy oatmeal, then topped with dog biscuit candles. If your dog is into sharing, you can invite over a few canine buddies.

* A **personalized denim dog bed** ($44–120, L.L. Bean, 800-221-4221).

* **Dog bone cookie cutters**, one large and one small, that come with two tasty recipes ($3, A Child's Dream, 800-359-2906).

* **A certificate for pet-sitting**, so the owners will not have to board their pet when they go away.

* **Bite the Man**, an adorable human-shaped fleece chew toy for man's best friend ($6, Restoration Hardware, call 800-762-1005 for the store nearest you). Wrap it in a snappy red bandanna kerchief.

#$1###

bets. **Giant jigsaw puzzles** with oversized pieces are fun, long-lasting gifts. For kids who are just learning to tell time, get *The Real Mother Goose Clock Book* ($6.95, Cartwheel Books), which has a built-in clock face with movable hands.

Community Playthings (800-777-4244) is a good catalog to check out for top-quality **solid maple play equipment** including a **nursery rocking boat** ($165), **building blocks, rocking chairs**, an **adjustable easel** with a chalk board and paint tray ($105), an **old-fashioned scooter** ($100), and a child-sized **wheelbarrow** ($90). The prices are not inexpensive, but these are gifts that will be passed down to the next generation. I am impressed with the integrity and thoughtfulness this company brings to their product line.

A **cassette player** (Sony makes a good one in the $30 range) with **music and books on tape** is an essential part of growing up and will be useful for years to come. Some tapes to consider: the *Wee Sing Silly Songs* series; **the music of Raffi**; Walt Disney's classics, including *101 Dalmatians*, and later, *The Secret Garden, Alice in Wonderland*, and *Wind in the Willows*; Roald Dahl's books; and at about eleven or twelve, classics like *Rebecca, Black Beauty*, and *The Hound of the Baskervilles*. By hearing them, rather than seeing them on TV, children can form their own images of the characters. What a great way to learn to appreciate literature!

You can ask grandparents to **tape bedtime stories** for their grandchild, made-up or read from a book. It will help to keep the generations connected even if distance separates them. Grandparents can record the story, and send the tape and the book to their grandchild, who can follow along. They can even record a funny noise to indicate when it's time to turn the page. When the child grows older, she can reciprocate and record a story for the grandfolks.

Gardening together is one of the nicest ways to pass time and learn with a child; digging in the fragrant earth, discovering bugs and worms, planting seeds, pulling weeds, and harvesting a meal. All the lessons of patience and nurturing can be found right in the backyard. Seeds of Change (888-329-4762) has some great gifts for the growing gardener, like small-sized, lightweight tools, made of hardwood and steel, instead of plastic, so they can really do the job, rather than break after a few uses. The **rake, hoe**, and **shovel** are priced right at $7.95 each, and make a fine gift individually or as a set. They also sell tough **children's gloves** for $6.95, a **bright red, small, sturdy steel watering can** for $12, and a dandy **bug collecting house** for $6.95. Many of their seeds are also good kid gifts; to encourage early gardening success, choose **large seeds** (beans, corn, peas, sunflowers), which are easier for small hands to handle and tend to germinate more reliably.

Kids love to grow **carnivorous plants** such as Venus's Flytraps and Pitcher Plants. They learn a little basic botany while marveling at the strange properties of these unusual plants, which are available at some garden centers and occasionally at the grocery store.

Find an **old trunk** (be sure to install a special hinge to prevent the lid from slamming on little fingers), spiff it up with a paint job and some stencils, and start a costume collection. Solicit donations from grandparents and other relatives to this repository for masks, scarves, capes, fabric, makeup, old belts, gloves, and hats. It'll provide years of fun when kids want to play dress-up or need to be outfitted for the class play. The trunk and its contents may be passed down to the children's children someday, and what a special gift that would be!

Little kids feel unique when they receive a personalized gift. The people at Create-a-Book (800-598-1044) will customize their books to include not only your child's name, but all sorts of details like friends' names, hometown, and age, so it feels like the book was really written especially for the child. Titles include *My Birthday Surprise* and *My Birthday Wish*, as well as books about fishing, camping, sports, dinosaurs, and more (prices range from $9.95 to $14.95). If you're creative, you can **make your own personalized book**, and provide the story line and illustrations yourself.

Birthdays, Birthdays, Everywhere

Children between the ages of about three and eleven may be invited to a dozen or more birthday parties annually—not to mention their own. If you have a child in this age group, you know it is sometimes difficult to come up with consistently good gifts that won't break the bank. Set a limit of $8 to $12; spending more than that is no guarantee that the gift will be a hit, and it may make the parents feel obligated if you overspend. Consider shopping somewhere besides the toy store. Here are a few ideas:

✳ *Bookstores.* My youngest son is a passionate reader, and for years his signature gift has been a **book tailored to the child**. It could be a basketball almanac for a sports lover, a drawing book for a budding young artist, or a humorous book for someone who needs a little nudge with reading.

✳ *Art supplies stores.* Beginning with **finger paints, stickers, construction paper, glitter and glue**, then **colored pencils, watercolors** and **modeling clay**, and on to **calligraphy pens, oils** and **canvas**, there is no end to the possibilities. Head to your nearby art supply store, or call Daniel Smith, 800-426-6740, or Flax, 800-547-7778, whose catalogs have an amazing selection of **printmaking, sculpting, and painting sets**, and all sorts of other fun things. An **easel with a chalkboard on one side** will last for years and encourage kids to paint and draw. **How-to art books** are available for almost any medium, so check with your local bookseller. Encourage children to turn off the tube and be creative.

✳ *Office supplies stores.* A **dry-erase board and marking pens**, a **desk lamp**, an **electric pencil sharpener**, a **bulletin board**—all are gifts the child will enjoy now and for the next decade.

✳ *Nature, space, and science specialty stores.* At stores such as The Nature Company (800-227-1114), Natural Wonders (800-2WONDERS), and Star Magic (three locations in Manhattan and one in San Francisco, or shop on-line at www.starmagic.com), you'll find vast supplies of reasonably priced, clever, fun, learning-oriented items including **glow-in-the-dark stars, maps, gadgets**, and **creepy crawly animals**.

Sports Fans

The new super-sports stores springing up in the malls of America are your resource for one-stop shopping if the kids on your list are crazy about sports. For the basketball fan, you can find everything from a **basketball key chain** or **trading cards** to a free-standing **regulation-height hoop**. There are inexpensive **hoops that hook over a door** for inside use; kids love them. **Frisbees** are a great gift for almost any age, almost any time. And the good thing is, people who use them, lose them (or the dog chews them), so they can always use another. A **tetherball** will provide countless hours of enjoyment for kids four through ten; just be sure there is an outdoor location where the pole can be sunk. For those age ten and up, a doorway-mounted **chin-up bar** (about $15) will see years of use, several times daily. Most boys and some girls love them, and it's a great way to promote fitness. More gifts for the fitness-oriented: an old-fashioned **pogo stick**, a **miniature trampoline**, or a **jump rope**.

If you want to avoid a trip to the mall, there is a good catalog called *The Training Camp* (800-ATHLETE), which sells all sorts of sports training equipment just for kids. They have an extensive range of no-nonsense products for most sports. If you've got a fanatic in your family, or want to encourage involvement, this catalog is for you.

Nerf and **Koosh toys** of all kinds are kid pleasers, and parent pleasers, too, because their soft texture makes them less likely to break lamps, windows, or heads. You'll find a large variety at any good-sized toy store.

Tickets to a special sporting event can be purchased far in advance, and it'll give the child something to look forward to. If you're near a large city you can try for pro basketball, baseball, hockey, or football tickets; semi-pro and college games are also a lot of fun and more affordable. And don't forget girls' sports—women's varsity basketball is one of the most exciting games going. Get extra tickets for a parent, and perhaps a lucky friend or sibling.

If you're looking for a gift for a boy or girl between the ages of eleven and eighteen, chances are he or she skateboards, snowboards, surfs, or would like to. Gift ideas for devotees (or wannabes) include **skateboarding**, **surfing**, or **snowboarding videos** of their heroes, **books**, **tee-shirts, hats, shades, fins, watches, leashes**, and **boards** of all kinds. **Bags** are useful for the traveling boarder to carry surf and snowboards and all the gear. The necessary apparel includes **logo tee-shirts, surf shorts, rash guards, snowboarding pants, boots, beanie**, and **gloves. Surfing, snowboarding, and skateboarding magazines** can keep them involved with their sport all year long, even when it's not in season.

Gifts and More Gifts

Kids and water go hand-in-hand. For a summer birthday, pack a **gym bag with a beach towel, sunscreen**, and a **gift certificate for swimming lessons**. Any time of year **fill a basket with bubble bath**, a **bath toy, and bath crayons**.

It's hard to keep up with the latest in **computer and video games**, so if you have a child who's hooked on these, you might want to consult him. Some old favorites: *Sim City*, *Where in the World Is Carmen Sandiego?*, and *The Oregon Trail*.

Walkie-talkies will provide hours of outdoor fun for kids from about six to ten years of age ($12.99 and up, at most electronics stores). Don't forget the batteries, so they can be put to use right away.

Who'd have guessed the National Archives in Washington, D.C. (800-234-8861) would be a place to find cool gifts? They have several **historical posters**, including the famous Rosie the Riveter saying, "WE CAN DO IT!", and Uncle Sam's, "I WANT YOU," each for only $7.50. They also have reproductions of the **Constitution**, the **Bill of Rights**, and the **Declaration of Independence** printed in duotones on parchmentlike paper, $.75 each.

A **goldfish** is a gentle introduction to the fun and responsibility of having a real, live pet—as opposed to the digital pets now in vogue. Look for **Aqua Baby**, a Plexiglas cube that comes with five tiny fish and a year's worth of food. With this gift, or any other from the animal kingdom, it is wise to seek parental permission in advance.

For children six and up, consider a **ride in a hot air balloon**, accompanied by an adult, of course. This is not an inexpensive gift, but the price is usually discounted for kids, and they absolutely love it—so will you. To find a ballooning company in your area, look in the Yellow Pages under "Balloons-Manned."

Collections

All sorts of **collections** can be started with a gift: coins, dolls, baseball cards, hats, old keys, animal figurines, masks; an added bonus is that you'll know what to get next year. Start a **charm bracelet** for a young girl, and she'll end up with a treasure she'll keep forever.

The U.S. Postal Service has a toll-free number (888-STAMP FUN) you can call to receive *Stampers*, a magazine for the would-be junior philatelist filled with amazing stamp facts and info on how to become a Stamper. Through the magazine, you can buy all kinds of stamps and related items: a **Bug-Eye Magnifier** ($2), **Stamp Tattoos** ($4), and a lot of great **collectible stamps**. My eleven-year-old read the magazine and started collecting immediately. The magazine is free, so you could send it along with an assortment of fun stamps and a little cash to get them started with their new hobby.

At the Museum of Childhood in London, I once saw an exhibit of the most extraordinary dollhouses—exquisitely detailed Victorian mansions with each room perfectly appointed; some were wired for electricity, and one even had running water. The dollhouses in the *Little Pilgrims Catalog* (888-475-4767) come close to those I saw in London. They offer three different three-story Victorian models, handcrafted and handpainted, with wooden shingled roofs and detailed staircases. These are not cheap: $425 for the **Victorian Town House**, up to $2,295 for the thirteen-room **Queen Anne Mansion**, which stands over four feet high, and was inspired by a real-life mansion in San Francisco. The furnishings are comparatively inexpensive: a **felt-topped pool table with a set of cues and a cue rack**, a **stool**, and an **overhanging lamp** cost $19.95; and a **complete Victorian bathroom with pull-chain toilet, pedestal sink,** and **footed tub** for $11. If you've been searching for the ultimate doll house, look no further.

There are dolls and there are dolls, and then there are **American Girls**. All the young girls (ages five to eleven) I know are begging for them. The collection begins with an old-fashioned baby doll (surprisingly difficult to find these days) named **Bitty Baby**, continues with the historical series—**Felicity** (c.1774), **Kirsten** (c.1854), **Addy** (c.1864), **Samantha** (c.1904), and **Molly** (c.1944)— and ends with the **American Girl of Today**, available with the child's own skin color, hair color, and eye color. There are a multitude of accessories, right down to miniature books and pencils. There is also an *American Girl Club*, a magazine, and an interactive **CD-ROM**; it's a whole subculture. The dolls are collectible quality that girls will want to save for their own daughters. Available only through the *American Girl Catalog*, 800-845-0005.

Year-Round Gifts

Kids love magazine subscriptions. My eleven-year-old runs to the mailbox every day, in hopes of finding the latest issue of ***Sports Illustrated for Kids*** (800-633-8628). I have to hide ***Snowboarding*** (888-TWS-MAGS) from my fifteen-year-old until homework is completed. Other good bets include the National Wildlife Federation (800-822-9919) magazines, ***Your Big Backyard*** for younger children, and ***Ranger***

Rick for ages six to nine. For kids five to twelve there's ***Highlights*** (800-253-8688), and for kids eight to thirteen, try ***Stone Soup*** (a literary magazine by and for kids, including poetry, stories, book reviews, and art, and a photo of each young contributor, 800-447-4569).

Hit the Road

I jump at the opportunity for children to **travel**, whenever and wherever they can. Nothing could be more educational and full of important life lessons, and fun. For kids age nine and up—who are able to fly unaccompanied—a **gift to visit Grandma or a favorite cousin** will give them a soaring sense of independence.

Grandparents can take children on a trip with them, and give the parents a gift at the same time—a little break. A **cruise** can be especially fun, because there are a lot of activities geared just for kids, and grandparents won't be burdened with entertaining them full time.

Send a kid to camp! This can be a gift from parents, siblings, or a special relative. With so many great camps around, it's hard to choose. Our favorites in recent years have included circus camp, kayaking camp, baseball camp, surfing camp, and a general, all-purpose, old-fashioned camp in the mountains with tents, hiking, boating, and archery. If you're a grandparent who lives far away from the grandchildren, you can send them to camp in your area and tie it in with a summer visit to your house.

Party Time

When your child is asked to a big party, your gift can be to **videotape the event** for the parents, and present them with the finished product.

Paint-your-own-ceramic studios are springing up all over the country. This is a fun place to take a child for a private birthday date, or several children for a party. This can be a double treat because the children can take a gift home to mom that will last a lifetime. You select a piece (mug, plate, bowl, teapot, cookie jar, flower pot, picture frame), then paint and decorate it with glaze. The studio clear glazes, then fires the piece, and you can pick it up a week later.

For a more active group, have a birthday party at **an indoor rock-climbing gym**, or **go bowling**, **miniature golfing**, or **Rollerblading**.

Totally Teenagers

Perhaps the most appropriate gift for a thirteen-year-old is a DO NOT DISTURB **sign** for his room. Yes, it's sometimes a tough age, and definitely a challenge to shop for, but not impossible. First, a few don'ts. Don't buy clothes for teenagers, unless you know *exactly* what brand, style, size, and color. And even then it's risky. Don't buy music for teenagers, unless, as above, you know *exactly* which artist or group, which album, and whether to buy cassettes or CDs.

If you're shopping for your own kids, ask them directly what they want. It's great to have that surprise element in a gift, but it's even better to give a gift that will be used and appreciated. In the case of clothing and music, you're better off giving **gift certificates** (just make sure they're for the right stores!), so they can make their own selections. Kids always want more apparel. **Gift certificates to Patagonia** (800-638-6464), **Eastern Mountain Sports** (888-463-6367), or **Sports Authority** (888-LOOK-4-TSA) will probably be on target, but it depends on the kid. You can also consider **gift certificates for electronics stores, movie theaters, bookstores, video rentals, indoor rock climbing, ice cream, fast-food restaurants,** and **athletic shoe stores**.

To whet their appetite for travel, give them a good atlas, such as the *Hammond New Century World Atlas* ($29.95). If they have a particular destination in mind already, give a **travel guide** from the *Let's Go* series of guidebooks produced by Harvard students, the *On The Loose* series written by students at the Berkeley campus of the University of California, or the *Lonely Planet* books, which offer some off-the-beaten-track treks at affordable prices. These books are filled with the kind of information young people are looking for, like where to stay cheaply, rather than where to find a four-star restaurant. You could accompany the guidebook with a **ticket to the destination**, or a contribution toward it.

You can **give them a real-life adventure**, with a **gift certificate for bungee-jumping, hang-gliding, or an indoor rock climbing facility**. On a grander scale, consider a **trip with a group like Overseas Adventure Travel** (800-353-6262), **Echo Wilderness Company** (800-652-ECHO), or **Outward Bound** (800-243-8520).

Books can be the ideal gift for teens if they're related to a subject of personal interest, like sports, art, music, dance, or adventure. *The Secret Language of Birthdays* by Gary Goldschneider ($34.95, Penguin Books) is a fantastic book filled with astrology, numerology, and the tarot, all rolled into one. Teens will love it. A copy of the *I Ching*, **60 yarrow stalks** or **3 Chinese coins** to work the oracle, a **deck of tarot cards**, or a **visit to a palm reader or fortune teller** could be a novel and intriguing gift. I gave my son a book on interpreting dreams, which he and his friends have enjoyed consulting.

If the teenager in your life doesn't have a **pager**, consider giving him one. You'll find teens a lot easier to keep track of if you can beep them anytime. You get peace of mind and they get a gift they love, for a small monthly charge. Your home phone will be a lot quieter, too, because all their friends will call them on their pager. A **private telephone line**, an **answering machine**, a **cordless phone**, a **prepaid calling card**, or some of the phone services, like **call waiting**, are greatly appreciated by this age group.

For a teenager of driving age, you can wrap up a **Matchbox version of their dream car**. If your teenager enjoys building things, give him or her a **model of a car from the year of their birth**. Most toy stores have a great selection of ready-made and do-it-yourself kits.

The colorful assortment of bath and personal care products at The Body Shop appeals to teens. This environmentally friendly company started in London in 1976, and now has over 1,500 stores worldwide. Choose your own gift assortment and put it in one of their canvas drawstring totes or a wicker basket (either, $3). Some of the fun products include **Blue Corn Mask** ($9.95), **Pineapple Facial Wash** ($9.70), **Cucumber Cleansing Milk** ($4.90), **Carrot Moisture Cream** ($9.50), and a soft **Skin Chamois** ($4.95). All products are made of natural ingredients and involve no animal testing. (Call 800-BODYSHOP to find the store nearest you or to order a catalog.)

Photographic equipment is a practical gift for teenagers, and something they will use for years to come. Possibilities include: a **basic point-and-shoot**, a **disposable underwater** or **wide-angle camera**, a **digital camera**, a **camcorder**, **film**, a **camera bag**, a **photo album**, and **frames**.

As you may have noticed, teenagers love music. You can encourage them by giving a **musical instrument**—anything from an **electric** or **acoustic guitar** to a **harmonica** or **drum**, or **accessories** to go with an instrument they own: **guitar picks**, a **new amplifier**, a **tuner**, a **music stand**, or **sheet music**. A **gift certificate** to Tower Records (800-648-4844), while not terribly personal, will probably be used immediately.

Guitar or other **music lessons** are a great gift. Other lessons to consider are **surfing, tennis**, or **golf. Classes in dance, rock climbing,** or **scuba diving** will help them perfect a skill and keep them busy.

One twenty-three-year-old I know gave her high school–aged sister a **college application tool kit** which included college catalogs, a monthly planner, a filing system, scholarship information, and a journal for college visits. Little sister was thrilled with this thoughtful gift.

Teens usually have more things to spend money on than ready cash at hand, so **monetary gifts** of all kinds are appreciated. They can take the form of **cash tucked into a new wallet or change purse;** a **savings bond** (one with a $50 face value costs $25); a **stock certificate;** or a crisp, new **$20, $50, or $100 bill trapped inside a plexiglas puzzle called a Money Maze** (The Lighter Side, 941-747-2356).

You can amuse yourself, and possibly your teenager, by assembling a **collection of small gifts, one for each letter in his or her name.** For example, for my son, Spencer, I could give **snowboarding cash** for *S*, a **Pilot pen** for *P*, **electric pencil sharpener** for *E*, **nail clippers** for *N*, a **Bob Marley CD** for *C*, an **art gum eraser** for *E*, and a **razor** for *R*.

If there is one thing that can be said about teenagers universally, it is that they are always hungry. A gift of his own **side of ribs and a quart of barbecue sauce, flown in from Texas,** goes a long way toward reconciling my son to our normally meatless diet. After devouring the ribs, and sharing them all around, he uses the sauce for the next two weeks on everything from omelets to pizza. I'd say this much satisfaction for $25 is quite a bargain (The Iron Works Barbecue, 800-669-3602).

Kids who are away at boarding school, camp, or college will also appreciate **food gifts**—the more the better, anytime, and especially on their birthdays. **Homemade chocolate chip cookies** lead the list. If they're away on their birthday you can **send them a birthday cake** from Piece of Cake (800-922-5390). A few other ideas:

* Stereo equipment
* Cellular phone
* Concert tickets
* CD or cassette carrying case
* Scented candles
* Gift certificate to have her photograph taken
* Incense
* Flowers
* Balloons
* Manicure
* **Admission to a laser light show** at the planetarium
* Boxers
* Barbells
* Lava Lamp
* Duffel bag for sports gear
* Magazine subscriptions *(Sports Illustrated, Snowboarding, Sassy, Popular Mechanics, Seventeen, Rolling Stone, Thrasher, Bust)*
* *Far Side* calendar
* Lift tickets for snowboarding or skiing
* Boom box
* Makeover
* Shaving gear
* Prepaid gasoline credit card
* Globe

Twenty-Somethings

Although this age group has definitely graduated to adulthood, their tastes may not be quite the same as those of a forty-year-old. Most twenty-somethings will be finishing school, getting jobs, and settling in to more permanent quarters—many of the suggestions in the "House-warming" chapter (page 56) will apply. See also the section on Graduation in "Rites of Passage" (page 120), which suggests gifts for those leaving home for the first time. They'll appreciate not only the basics, but also the aesthetic touches that make a house a home, such as a **vase with a note encouraging them to indulge in a weekly treat of cut flowers**.

Another great gift for a special twenty-something on your list is a subscription to the **International Herald Tribune** (800-842-2884). It delivers top-quality news in a distilled fashion that is more compatible with their fast-paced lives than a fat, multisectioned, city newspaper might be.

Gifts for Grownups

At a certain age, birthdays cease to be as significant as they were in childhood; one year rolls into the next without any dramatic change. Some people see birthdays as an unwanted reminder of the inexorable process of aging, and would rather not take notice. Nevertheless, for one day a year it is our special day, and we like to be celebrated. Gifts are not always necessary. I love receiving **phone calls** from local and faraway friends who want to remember me on my birthday; that simple gesture means a lot.

Who wouldn't enjoy **birthday breakfast in bed**? Delivered on a beautiful tray, with a copy of the *New York Times* or his favorite newspaper, fresh orange juice and coffee, serve up your specialty, his favorite, or something scrumptious like yeasty buckwheat pancakes with warm maple syrup and caramelized apples. If you want to avoid last-minute cooking, put together the best scones you can find in a basket with lemon curd and raspberry jam. This is a great gesture to make for a spouse, but even more fun to give someone you don't live with, because of the surprise element.

How about a **journal**? Kate's Paperie in New York is famous for their vast assortment of over 4,000 papers, but they are also known for their very fine **photo albums** and journals. A perennial favorite is the **Firenze journal**, made in the 16th-century Florentine style, of soft, buttery leather with a long leather thong for closure.

Kate's also has an extensive collection of **writing instruments**, including the well-known **Waterman** and **Mont Blanc pens**, as well as pens imported from Italy, Germany, and France. The current star is the **Cesare Emiliano pen**, in a range of colors with a resin body and a sterling silver tip, available in ballpoint, roller ball, or fountain pen ($100 to $160). If you can't make it to one of their stores, call for their catalog (800-809-9880).

For the grown-up in your life who never grew up, or for the person who needs a little help remembering how to play, collect a **box full of toys**. This is one of those gifts that is almost as much fun to give as to receive. Choose the things you would have loved when you were ten: **magnets, jacks**, a **yo-yo**, a **Slinky**, a **gyroscope**, a **kite**, a **balsa wood airplane**. Are there women out there besides me who always wanted an **Easy-Bake Oven**, with the tiny pans and the real, miniature mixes?

When a friend in another city is having a birthday, you can call and **have dinner sent in** if you know the restaurant scene in their part of the world. An ex–New Yorker I know loves to surprise the folks back home with Japanese takeout. Her friends are bowled over, and the restaurant gets a kick out of receiving a call from the other coast for delivery service.

As a gift to a friend, **invite her to attend a class with you**, and you cover the cost of tuition. This can be a one-night event, or a semester-long course. Cooking, art history, martial arts, yoga, paper making, financial planning—it's always more fun with two.

Nature lovers will appreciate a good pair of **binoculars** and **guidebooks of all kinds: birds, trees, spiders, wildflowers**. There are also many beautiful books with stunning photos of animals and nature scenes; explore the possibilities at your local bookstore. Other outdoor enthusiasts might enjoy **a telescope** and a copy of H. A. Rey's classic, ***The Stars***. While technically classified as a juvenile book, it will appeal to anyone who wants to look at the night sky in a new way.

It is always a thoughtful gesture to **frame an important document**: a degree, certificate, or honor, and wrap it up as a birthday gift. This is one of those things we seldom get around to doing for ourselves, and it's a very personal gift.

Chances are, a movie buff will already own most of **his favorite videos**, but if not, you can wrap up a few with a **supply of popcorn** and a copy of the ***Videohound Guide to Three- and Four-Star Movies*** ($10.99, Broadway Books), the ultimate guide to the best movies of all time.

Almost anyone, regardless of age, will enjoy a copy of ***Life* magazine** from the week of their birth. These are available for the years 1940 to 1972, and must be ordered 4–6 weeks ahead of time ($20, The Lighter Side, 941-747-2356). You can also shop for a **model of an automobile from their birth year** at your local hobby or toy store. A **bottle of wine of the same vintage** may be harder to find, depending upon the age of the recipient.

I know a man who sends his mother-in-law **flowers every year** on his wife's birthday, to thank her for mothering his mate. I don't need to tell you that she thinks he's pretty great. This sort of gesture will go a long way toward solving your mother-in-law problems.

Thoughtful books make thoughtful gifts. I love to receive gifts from friends, because I know they've been selected especially with me in mind. *A Painter's Garden—Cultivating the Creative Life* by Christine Walker ($18.95, Warner Books) discusses gardening and painting as a means of unlocking creativity, and is filled with the author's luscious paintings. It is perhaps especially appropriate for a woman to give to a woman, as is *Creative Companion: How to Free Your Creative Spirit* by Sark ($12.95, Celestial Arts). *Don't Sweat the Small Stuff . . . And It's All Small Stuff* by Richard Carlson ($10.95, Hyperion) will appeal to almost everyone who would like to relax and live more peacefully.

Senior Birthdays

Many people who have no trouble choosing gifts for most of the people in their lives find it difficult to shop for their parents, grandparents, or other senior citizens. Older people have different needs and wishes when it comes to gifts. Most are no longer in the acquisitive stage of life. In fact, for many, it is a time of letting go of material possessions after a lifetime of accumulation. They don't want one more dust catcher, so how can you show them you care without heaping more useless objects on their knickknack shelf?

Rather than giving them material things, think in terms of occasions you can help create: **dinner**, a **party**, a **ball game, the ballet, outings of all kinds,** depending on their mobility and interests. Your gift of an evening out could become a new annual tradition.

Also remember when giving to the elderly to make sure the gift is complete. If you're giving something related to a hobby or activity,

Gifts for Seniors

* **Stationery**, **postcards**, and **an assortment of cards** for various occasions, along with a lot of stamps.

* **Gift certificate for a cleaning service.**

* **An invitation to dinner or a movie.**

* **Gift certificate for a handyman** to visit the house.

* **Cozy things:** sheepskin slippers, a wool muffler, a hot water bottle, fuzzy socks.

* **Monthly gardening or landscaping service.**

* **A cordless phone,** preprogrammed with telephone numbers for emergency services and family members.

* **A regularly scheduled phone call that they can count on.**

* **The *New York Times*, large-type weekly** (6 months for $30, 800-631-2580).

* A **cookie jar filled with homemade cookies.**

* **Magazine subscriptions** (A few that might appeal:*Smithsonian*, 800-766-2149; *Sunset*, 800-777-0177; *Golf Digest*, 800-PAR-GOLF; or *Audubon*, 800-274-4201).

* **Good-tasting and nutritious meals delivered to the door.**

include all the necessary components. It might be difficult for them to get out and buy batteries for the tape player, or to locate the right pump for the aquarium you've chosen. If you're giving them a bird feeder, include a birder's guidebook, and some birdseed.

Older people love to be pampered, but often don't know how. The *Self-Care Catalog* (800-345-3371) offers several possibilities for pampering and therapeutic gifts: a **Bed Lounge easy chair**, filled with feathers and down, for reading in bed ($130); an **electric foot or back massager** that actually squeezes sore muscles ($260); and a **paraffin bath** for aching joints ($180).

There is a wonderful book, ***Legacy: a Step-by-Step Guide to Writing a Personal History*** ($14.95, Swallow Press), which you could give to encourage the process of unlocking memories. It was written by Linda Spence after she asked her mother to write her life story, and her mother replied, "How? Where do I begin?" As the author points out, a personal history is a gift to share, and one that can restore the connection between generations.

You could also give an **easy-to-operate tape recorder** (Sony makes one in the $30 range). Be sure to include batteries and several blank cassettes. Your card can say something to the effect of, "Our gift to you is this tape recorder. We hope you'll give us the gift of your family stories." Include a list of prompts to get them started, such as, "Tell us about summers on the lake," or, "Describe the town you grew up in," or, "Talk about how you and dad met." It might be hard for them to begin, but once they do, they'll be on their way to writing their memoirs and spending hours enjoying reminiscence. It's a good way to ease loneliness, too.

Books on tape are a thoughtful gift if failing eyesight is a problem. Choose from hundreds of titles in all categories: history, biography, best-sellers, mystery, humor—all available through Audio Editions, 800-231-4261. Or give them a collection of **tapes from favorite vintage radio shows**: Jack Benny, Burns & Allen, Sam Spade, Jimmy Stewart as the Six-Shooter, and much more, available from Adventures in Cassettes, 800-328-0108.

Some elderly people are intimidated by all the new technology, so a really thoughtful gift could be to give them a **computer**; along with some basic instruction on its use, to ease their fears. A **subscription to**

America Online (800-827-6361) or **another internet service provider** will help you to stay in contact with one another regularly via E-mail, and they'll be linked with the rest of the world through the World Wide Web.

If they have not kept up with telephone technology recently, they'll be delighted with a **cordless phone,** particularly if you've pre-programmed it with emergency and family phone numbers. Make sure the model you buy has a handset locator on the base, so they can find the phone in case they forget where they last used it— it happens to everyone!

If your senior friend is a radio listener, you can **request a birthday greeting or a special song on their favorite station**, and make sure they're tuned in to hear it.

Milestones

Landmark birthdays, twenty-one, thirty, forty, fifty, sixty-five, one hundred, call for gifts of significance. The present does not need to be costly, but should, in some way, be symbolic.

You might think of giving **forty, fifty, or a hundred of some small object: golf balls, cigars, ice cream cone gift certificates, paperwhite narcissus bulbs, silver dollars, sea shells. Forty helium balloons** can make quite a statement. A friend gave her niece **thirty miniature troll dolls**, in memory of her childhood collection; because it was so personal and funny, it was her favorite gift. Or **give a gift for each decade**: a fiftieth birthday can be marked with **five antique rose bushes, or five books.**

Order a **gigantic banner** from Supergram (800-3-BANNER) for a personalized greeting on an important birthday. They'll help you out with ideas for the message.

I attended a fortieth birthday bash a few years ago where the guest of honor received from his partner a beautiful package. The guests exclaimed as he unwrapped a breathtaking bronze statue of a horse. Then he found the real gift: beneath the statue were the registration papers for a **black stallion colt**. The gift was a memorable combination of cleverness and extravagance.

If you have a friend who is turning forty, get several friends to chip in for **race car driving classes**. Guys love it, and possibly it'll help to keep that midlife crisis at bay. (Call a racetrack near you, or look in the Yellow Pages under "Driving Schools" or "Racing Schools.")

I was surprised one year by the gift of a **ride and lesson in a glider.** I was touring around the English countryside with a friend; suddenly he turned off the road and there it was! The gift was thrilling, the surprise was even better.

Another friend chose a unique way to celebrate her fortieth. She had recently moved and lived at a distance from most of her friends, so she wrote a letter to everyone about a month before her birthday, asking each of us to send her a **memory**. She wrote that she would find a special place on her birthday and read each of our offerings. Some were silly, some were poignant, she laughed and cried, and felt like she'd been truly celebrated by her friends, even though she spent the day alone.

A friend who turned sixty chose a similar way to mark the occasion. She knew she would be out of the country with her family on the special day, and thus unable to celebrate with her friends, so she asked each of them to give her a **little wisdom** to carry her into her next decade. She took time on her birthday to open her gifts of wisdom, which took many forms, from small talismans to original poetry.

Some people plan physical feats to celebrate milestone birthdays. One woman I know hiked to the bottom of the Grand Canyon, then had the best suite (with jacuzzi) in the hotel waiting for her when she completed her climb out of the canyon.

For a friend turning fifty who has a little trepidation about aging, you can assemble a **semiserious**, **semigag gift basket**, including reading glasses, a pen that hangs around the neck, a magnifying glass, a flashlight, because "most activities require more light at this age," and a book along the lines of *Is It Hot In Here, or Is It Just Me?* a book about menopause by Gayle Sand ($13, HarperPerennial).

For his fiftieth birthday, a friend gave her husband a **croquet party** at an exclusive resort in the wine country of California. The guests, looking elegant in white, sipped champagne, and played at being Gatsby for a few hours. He'd always imagined such a gathering; she made his dream come true.

A friend planned a seventieth birthday party for her dad, and arranged to **have a woman jump out of the cake.** This might not be appropriate for some people, but he loved it.

You can **throw a party** for an older friend or relative celebrating a significant birthday, and invite all her friends. Take photographs of the event, and get a shot of the guest of honor with each of the party-goers. Afterward, have several copies of each print made and put together small albums to send to each of the guests, and a more elaborate one for the birthday celebrant.

For the eightieth birthday, and all those that follow, you can **request that a card be sent from the mayor, the governor, or the President.** Why not all three? You can hardly have too many birthday greetings. To request the President's best wishes, write to the Greetings Office at the White House, Washington, DC 20500, and provide the recipient's name, address, and date of birth.

Birthdays by the Month

Following is a list of traditional birthstones and flowers, which may guide you in your choice of gifts. **Birthstone rings** are available at many jewelers, or you can get miniature half-inch sterling silver rings, set with gemstones, to be worn on a sterling silver chain (ring, $20; chain, $12, Signals, 800-669-9696).

Month	Birthstone	Flower
January	garnet	carnation
February	amethyst	violet
March	bloodstone	daffodil
April	diamond	daisy
May	emerald	lily-of-the-valley
June	pearl	red rose
July	ruby	larkspur
August	sardonyx	poppy
September	sapphire	aster
October	opal	calendula
November	topaz	chrysanthemum
December	turquoise	holly

2

Weddings and Anniversaries

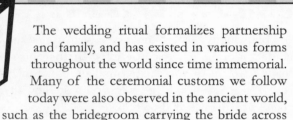

The wedding ritual formalizes partnership and family, and has existed in various forms throughout the world since time immemorial. Many of the ceremonial customs we follow today were also observed in the ancient world, such as the bridegroom carrying the bride across the threshold of their home. Trends come and go, but regardless of how the momentous event is observed, it is always an occasion for celebration.

Engagements

For many years engagement gift giving was out of fashion, sometimes kept alive, like so many other traditions, by the elders of the family. I have a friend whose ninety-five-year-old grandmother gives each of her grandchildren an **Irish damask linen tablecloth** from a little shop in Dublin on the occasion of their engagement. My friend has yet to use her tablecloth, but she treasures it above everything she owns because of the tradition it embodies, which she plans to carry on with her own grandchildren someday.

Lately there has been a return to this custom of honoring the engagement. Gifts need not be costly—a small token like a **book** or a **charm** will let the bride-to-be know you are thinking of her. You will be buying a wedding gift and possibly a shower gift as well, so budget accordingly. Gifts usually are directed to the bride and might include **bath** or **kitchen towels, bed linens,** and **lingerie. Cards** and **flowers** are also appreciated—everyone can contribute to making this a very special time of life.

The groom's present to his bride is traditionally the **engagement ring,** and the bride sometimes chooses a small personal gift for the groom, such as a **handsome watch** or a **beautifully framed photograph** of herself. In France, the families of the betrothed couple mark the occasion with an **exchange of bouquets;** I think this is a beautiful gesture of friendship and congratulations.

A few months prior to the wedding, an **engagement party** may be held. These range in terms of style and size, from a casual pot luck get-together to a black tie affair, and serve as a way for the family and friends of the future bride and groom to get better acquainted. If you're invited to an engagement party, or simply wish to express your happiness at the couple's good fortune, a small gift from the bridal registry is appropriate. One sweet gift for the bride is a **Limoges box,** in which she can place her rings. Celebration Fantastic, 800-CELE-BRATE, carries a wide and whimsical selection to suit all different tastes.

Bridal Showers

Like baby showers, bridal showers began as a way to prepare a young woman for the household management she would soon undertake. Traditionally, shower gifts were handmade, and these are still the nicest ones. Today, showers are often given for the bridal couple together, and the shower is a coed affair, with gifts along the lines of wedding presents, except less expensive. Typically, the hostess gives the shower guests a small favor, like a **pansy planted in a stenciled flower pot,** or **candles tied with ribbons of the bridal colors.**

These days, shower gifts are often purchased off the bridal registry list. Typical gifts include **candlesticks, towels, linens, pots** and **pans,** or **bar accessories.** If it's on the registry, you can be assured that the bride and groom genuinely do want the item, but if you are searching for something a little more unique, why not **frame the shower invitation** as a gift? Another gift that is sure to add some fun to the shower is *The Newlyweds' Predictionary* ($19.95, Andrews & McMeel), dubbed "a safe-deposit of hopes, plans, promises, and expectations of your first ten years together." The idea is the bride and groom independently fill out an extensive questionnaire filled with amusing and thought-provoking questions. It also includes thirty scaled-down questionnaires intended for family and friends, which can be completed at the shower. Then, the whole package is sealed up, not to be opened until the tenth anniversary, when they can examine what everyone (including their younger selves) predicted for them.

As with all gifts, those that are handmade seem to mean the most. One friend was given a **cookbook of favorite recipes** compiled by another friend whose cooking and baking is legendary. This is the one cookbook she really trusts and uses all the time.

Showers are often themed: a popular one is the round-the-clock shower, whereby each guest is assigned one of the twenty-four hours in the day and asked to bring a gift that would be used at that time. A shower for a couple of film buffs can have a movie theme, and gifts can be **additions to their video library**. Wine aficionados can be feted with **contributions to a wine cellar**. Those giving the shower can discuss with the couple what they might like or need—if household goods are in short supply, a **kitchen** or **bathroom shower** may be most helpful. My idea of heaven is a **book** or **music shower**.

One fun part about showers is the exchange of advice. Whether the topic is cooking, cleaning, sex, or who takes out the garbage, chances are at a females-only shower the bride will receive a whole load of advice on all the topics covered. One nice thought is to **videotape the event** or provide a journal in which the attendees can express their good wishes, hopes, and love for the couple.

A females-only gathering might be designated as a **lingerie shower**, and if you are shopping for a gift, it's best to have a clear idea of the bride's sizes. Avoid anything with an exacting fit, so she won't have to spend her time exchanging the wrong size. If you're unsure of size, choose something loose fitting, such as a **robe** or **nightgown**. Anything in silk is sublime: a **camisole**, **teddy**, **panties**, **stockings**, **night-**

gown, garter belt, boxers for her, or a lingerie case. A good source is Victoria's Secret. To request a catalog or find out the nearest location of one of their 366 stores, call 800-888-1500.

A unique gift that is appropriate before the wedding is **ballroom dancing lessons.** It's an art that few young people today have mastered. With enough practice, they'll be waltzing away their wedding night and may even keep up the hobby after the wedding.

Some additional fun shower gifts include:

✳ Any **parlor game**, from chess to Risk. Providing the couple has an imagination, the games could take on a whole new meaning.

✳ The cookbook ***Food as Foreplay: Recipes for Romance, Love and Lust*** (Alexandria Press). Food can be a powerful aphrodisiac, and this book unlocks the secrets of turning a humdrum dinner into Nirvana.

✳ **Beautiful and elegant writing paper** to be used for love letters only. Maybe they'll use it to write thank you notes, but if your instructions come with the book (see *How to Write Love Letters,* page 80) they'll get the hint.

✳ A **large, beautiful blank book**. In it, the couple can express their love, remind each other to buy milk, plan their dream house—whatever. Something about blank pages stimulates creativity, and if your note to the couple includes instructions to use this in their daily life, it may become a habit.

For the Bridal Party

Tradition holds that gifts be given by the bridal couple to the wedding attendants, in appreciation of their support. The Elizabethan custom was that bridesmaids were given **silk scarves** and groomsmen **fine gloves** as tokens of gratitude from the bride and groom. The gift needn't be costly, particularly if you have several attendants and a tight budget, but whatever you choose, it should be something long-lasting.

The ushers and best man are usually given their gifts at the bachelor party, which they hold in honor of the groom. Another opportunity for gift exchange is at the rehearsal dinner, hosted by the groom's parents. Classic gifts include **cuff links**, an **engraved silver pen**, an **engraved** flask, or **engraved bar glasses or accessories**. Sports fans may appreciate **tickets to an NFL, NBA, or NHL game. Good cigars** and **cigar accessories** are popular; see a list of great gifts for the cigar lover on page 151. For a more casual guy, a **picture frame** or a **wallet** are appropriate.

A thoughtful way for the bride to say thank you to her bridesmaids is to treat them to a **day** or **half-day at a spa** a week before the wedding. Everyone will be in need of a little R&R by then, and this is a nice way to relax and share the excitement together, while pampering yourselves. You will probably want to **have a bachelorette party** to coincide with the bachelor party and give gifts to your attendants then. You can "do lunch," or something a little more out of the ordinary, like **go ice-skating, rent a limo for a night on the town**, or **have an elegant tea party**, complete with cucumber sandwiches and scones, strawberry jam, and Devon cream. A **jewelry box**, an **engraved silver compact**, or a **charm bracelet** are all enduring and thoughtful gifts. A **necklace** or **bracelet** to wear with the bridesmaid gown will be a lasting remembrance of the special day. A **claddagh ring**, with its symbolism— "heart for love, hands for service, and crown for loyalty"—may be particularly apt.

Another idea is to give the attendants a **photograph of the wedding party** or the **bridal couple**, in a frame engraved with the wedding date.

If you're looking for a favor for a bridal shower, the rehearsal dinner, or to give to the wedding guests, nothing could be nicer than the **miniature ballotins** from Godiva (800-9-GODIVA, set of four, $12), which contain a light- and a dark-filled chocolate heart. The signature gold foil box is topped with a white rose. Perhaps not as elegant, but a whole lot more fun, is to give a **bottle of bubbles** to everyone at the reception. Another inexpensive gift for the guests is a **heart-shaped cookie**, wrapped in cellophane and tied with a bow.

Wedding Presents

It's best to send a gift as soon as you receive the wedding invitation, but it is acceptable to send it up to a year after the wedding. Don't overlook the possibility of giving **cash**. Money is always an appropriate wedding gift, and far from being in poor taste, this can be the best possible choice for a young couple saving for a down payment, for example.

The value of the present you select, cash or otherwise, depends upon your means, as well as your relationship to the couple. You shouldn't feel as though you have to give an expensive gift; there are many possibilities that are very affordable, like a **caviar server** made of horn (Dandelion, 888-548-1968), a perfect little wedding gift for only $5, or an elegant and inexpensive pair of tiny **cut crystal salt bowls and silver spoons**, in a blue velveteen bag ($12, Restoration Hardware, 800-762-1005).

In the case of a formal wedding, the attendants may want to join together to give the bride and groom a gift, such as **his and her watches**, a **leather photo album**, a **clock**, **monogrammed bar glasses**, or a **tray** engraved with their signatures and the wedding date. Tiffany's (800-526-0649) has a small silver tray that can be etched with the wedding invitation ($335).

The groom's family traditionally gives a gift of jewelry to the bride. This gift can be a **watch**, a **gemstone brooch**, **earrings**, or a **silver or gold bracelet**. Their gift might be part of the traditional "something old, something new, something borrowed, something blue, and a silver sixpence in your shoe"—like an **heirloom locket**, or a **string of pearls**. **Sixpence** were last minted in England in 1967, but you can still get one from Harrod's in London. The bride slips it into her shoe before she walks down the aisle, to ensure an abundance of prosperity and good fortune in the marriage.

If you are a parent or relative of the bridal couple, a **family heirloom** or something linked to a family tradition may be the most treasured gift you can give. This could include a set of fine **sterling silverware**, an **antique bed**, a **work of art**, or an **antique dresser**.

Before you decide on a wedding gift, ask where the bride and groom have registered in a bridal registry. They will probably register their preferences in one or two stores, and they will probably include items in a wide price range. If you choose from what they've selected, you'll know that you're giving them something they want, and if not, at least you may have a better idea of their tastes and what direction to take. Many young couples register at Crate and Barrel (800-967-6696), and even if they're not registered there, it's a good place to look for less expensive, good quality kitchen and houseware gifts. Other good bets include Williams-Sonoma, Macy's, and Pottery Barn.

If it's a first wedding for a young couple, think about practical gifts such as **furniture**; **linens for bed**, **bath**, and **table**; and kitchen essentials such as **pots and pans** and **small appliances**. They will want help with the basics of setting up a household before they begin to acquire decorative accessories. Your gift can be equally wonderful whether it is from Tiffany's or the hardware store. By far the best-loved and most useful piece in my *batterie de cuisine* is a ten-inch **cast-iron skillet**, which goes for about $13.

When in doubt, Tiffany's (800-526-0649) is a veritable treasure trove of classic wedding gifts. Their signature blue box always carries with it a certain cachet, and your gift will be remembered. Choose from a boxed set of **individual salt and pepper shakers** in sterling and vermeil ($150), a **brass clock** ($100), **crystal candlesticks** ($35–65), a **crystal ice bucket** ($45), or a set of **crystal champagne flutes** ($16 each). A **sterling silver frame** ($145) can be engraved and used to hold a wedding photograph of the bridal couple.

Bergdorf Goodman's most popular wedding registry item is the Hotel Collection of silver plate. Bergdorf's buys vintage pieces from hotels and ocean liners—such as **tea services**, **platters**, **tureens**, and **serving pieces**—then offers them for sale. Even if the bridal couple is not registered at Bergdorf's, they would probably love to receive a piece of old silver, and it will go well with whatever they have—silver is always in style. The staff can help you over the phone, as well as sending photographs of the particular pieces you are interested in. Bergdorf's offers a simple, sturdy, and oversized custom **flatware pattern in silver plate** to go with the vintage pieces. **Hotel silver** bridges the gap between sterling and stainless: it is dishwasher-proof and can be used every day. Call their Client Services number (800-218-4918) and ask for the Hotel Collection.

For the beauty and tradition of silver without going to great expense, consider the **silver plate napkin rings** at Sur La Table ($4.95 each, 800-243-0852). Here you will also find a classic **stainless steel martini shaker** ($38.95) and a **cocktail stirrer and strainer** ($9.95 each).

A personalized **sterling silver cake server** can be used to cut the wedding cake, and ever after serve as a reminder of the day. You can find a sterling silver one at most fine department stores, or Dandelion has a less expensive one in silver plate, suitable for engraving ($20, 888-548-1968).

If the couple is just starting out, consider giving them a **household tool kit**. Include a good hammer, a measuring tape, a set of normal and Phillips head screwdrivers, wrenches—all in a serviceable, high quality toolbox. Your local hardware store manager can help you find just the right items. A **book on home repair** would be useful, too (see page 61).

Give the couple a **gift certificate for the wedding photography**. This idea is especially appropriate if there are budget constraints, and they might otherwise have to skimp. Be sure to check well in advance of the big day to make sure they haven't made other arrangements. A **special photo album** is also a good idea; you'll find a beautifully bound, handmade wedding album on-line at 911 Gifts (www.911gifts.com), and there are many in the marketplace.

You can **take snapshots at the wedding**, drop the film at a one-hour developer as soon as you leave the ceremony, then pick up the prints and put them in an album you've selected ahead of time, and give the finished product to the bride and groom in the receiving line. This will not be a substitute for the formal photos, but it'll be great fun.

One of my favorite gifts when I got married was the **invitations** themselves, produced by a friend who is a graphic designer. If you have any talent to contribute to the wedding in terms of goods and services: **flowers, catering, photography, videotaping, cake decorating, music**, the bridal couple will remember your gift forever. You could **sew the bridal gown, play your flute** during the ceremony, or handle the **table arranging** and centerpieces at the reception. If you are famous for preparing a particular dish, you can offer to make it for the guests, especially if it is an ethnic specialty which might add personal meaning to the event.

If you have a **vacation home** that might be the perfect setting for a romantic honeymoon, consider offering it as your gift. This is especially appropriate if the couple might not be able to afford a special honeymoon otherwise. You may offer your cabin or cottage for a **romantic getaway**, to be used by the couple in their first year of marriage.

Personalized stationery is making a comeback and would be cherished by any bridal couple, particularly if a change in name or residence is involved. Kate's Paperie in New York (800-809-9880) has one of the finest selections of paper anywhere and offers engraving, thermograph printing, and old-fashioned letterpress printing, done by hand. If you're not in New York, their expert staff can guide you through the selection process over the phone. Kate's extraordinary gift wrapping will make this a memorable present. For a less traditional approach, call Claudia Laub Studios in Los Angeles (213-931-1710). Ms. Laub's **hip stationery** is sold through several stores around the country, but go to the source for custom printing and the best selection.

Give the bridal couple a pair of **glass bedside carafe and drinking glass sets**, etched with "His" and "Hers" ($20 each, Dandelion, 888-548-1968).

Almost every couple can use one more **white platter**. They are available everywhere, but for the last word, and the best selection anywhere, visit or call Wolfman-Gold & Good Company, in New York (212-431-1888). They stock white platters in all shapes and sizes, plain or with a border, mostly priced from $45–100. They are a great source for tasteful, classic, and contemporary wedding gifts, including **cake stands**, **serving bowls**, **soup tureens**, and the like. There is a whimsical **silver plate toast caddy** that spells out T-O-A-S-T, and a **rack for letters** that spells out L-E-T-T-E-R-S. They also offer an incredible collection of **bird houses**, some of them one-of-a-kind, ranging in price from $40–600. Even if the couple are not bird fanciers, these make great interior accents.

The enduring popularity of the **Baccarat crystal stemware** design, "Capri," may be a result of the beloved Princess Grace having chosen it for her pattern when she married Prince Rainier of Monaco, more than forty years ago. If it's good enough for the prince and princess, well . . . I'll never forget the story a friend recounts of watching eight Baccarat champagne flutes go down in one fell swoop when the tray-carrying hostess tossed her heavy braid. Baccarat also features countless other crystal pieces with timeless appeal (800-777-0100).

You don't have to go the traditional route of sterling, china, and crystal, if the couple you are shopping for are not that type. Laminate some particularly outrageous cover pages from the *National Enquirer* or the *Star*, and give them as a set of **place mats**, along with a collection of **wind-up toys**, or **push-bottom puppets**, to keep the dinner conversation lively.

The Asprey name is synonymous with impeccable gifts. Not long after they moved to New Bond Street in 1847, they were granted the Royal Warrant from Queen Victoria and have been serving royalty and other well-heeled Londoners ever since. It remains essentially what it was when it was founded: a family business specializing in luxury goods. Shopping for the bridal couple can begin and end here, if *budget* is not a word in your vocabulary. Consider the **willow picnic hamper** with brass and English bridle leather fittings, fully outfitted with Royal Grafton china, crystal tumblers, stainless steel cutlery, salt and pepper pots in light oak, Irish linen napkins, and stainless steel flasks and food containers ($1,200 for two, $1,650 for four), or perhaps the **hammered sterling martini goblets** ($750), the classically styled **silver-plated watering can** ($185), or the fully bound **green goatskin photograph album** ($115). Their motto, "It can be done," should be refreshing in today's retail world, where "customer service" has become a euphemism for the complaint department. Asprey takes great pride in honoring unusual requests.

If the Asprey picnic basket sounds a little pricey, **a more modest version** can be found at Brookstone ($250, 800-351-7222). The set includes service for four packed in a willow basket with leather trim, English stoneware plates, stainless steel utensils, French bistro glasses, a checkered tablecloth and matching napkins, insulated wine carrier, corkscrew, three resealable food containers, and a wooden cheese board with a knife.

Or, **put together your own picnic basket**—every couple should have one. You can buy the basket at an import store and fill it with wine, glasses, a bottle opener, napkins, a picnic cloth, and a few non-perishable gourmet specialty foods to get them started: cookies, olives, smoked salmon—the choices can be dictated by their tastes and your budget.

For an affordable gift that will last a lifetime, order a **wool stadium blanket**, personalized with the couple's name or monogram and wedding date, from J. W. Bentley ($39–49, depending on color, 510-820-6648). It takes them only a few days to ship custom orders.

The bridal couple will probably have an opinion about pots and pans, but regardless of what they have chosen, a piece of **copper cookware**, or anything made of copper, will be treasured. Sur La Table (800-243-0852) has a beautiful but functional **copper colander** ($51.95) and many **copper utensils**.

Some personalized possibilities: a **brass door knocker** (several styles are available in the $25 price range from Lillian Vernon, 800-285-5555), **towels** and **monogrammed terry cloth robes** (Hammacher Schlemmer, 800-543-3366), or a **doormat** with the couple's new name.

A **subscription to the opera, theater**, or **symphony season** is a splendid gift for the sophisticated urban couple. A **pair of tickets** would do nicely, too, perhaps wrapped up with **opera glasses**, either new or antique. Start a **library of CDs**—Broadway show tunes, opera or classical—and add to it on future occasions, perhaps for an anniversary gift.

The **Menu of the Month** from Diamond Organics (888-ORGANIC) is an inspired gift for the working couple. Once a month they'll be sent a great dinner via FedEx. For example, March's menu is organic tagliarini pasta with leeks, parsnip, bell pepper, sage, and garlic; organic sourdough bread; mesclun salad; and pears. The December Holiday Platter includes pineapple guava and red pears; mandarins and fuyu persimmons; baby carrots, cucumbers, and radishes; cherry tomatoes, broccoli, and celery; veggie dip with herbs, and a sourdough rosemary baguette. Everything is organically grown, and harvested to order (prices vary).

Francis Ford Coppola, the famed movie director, found the **perfect pasta bowl** in a little bistro in Italy and now imports it exclusively for his Napa Valley winery, Niebaum-Coppola. You can assemble a gift of two bowls ($12 each), **Niebaum-Coppola pasta** (made using antique bronze dies to produce a coarse texture, which allows the sauce to cling), **Mammarella's Pasta Sauce** (custom-made according to Coppola's mother's recipe, $4.99), and a **bottle of his latest wine**, Francis Coppola Presents ($12). Call the winery at 707-968-1135.

Give the happy couple a **collection of wine** from the year they met, to start their wine cellar. With any luck, you'll be asked to drink a bottle with them.

Call Peet's Coffee in Berkeley and have them deliver a different pound of their incomparable **coffee every month for a year** (Peet's

Coffee, 800-999-2132). Or wrap up a pound of beans with a **Bodum French press coffee maker** ($20-45).

You can put together a **breakfast in bed collection** for the bride and groom, with a tray, coffee beans, an assortment of jams and honey, a few beautiful napkins, and a pair of cafe au lait bowls. Add your favorite recipes for scones, popovers, and biscuits, or a cookbook featuring breakfast goodies.

Start or add to their **library of cookbooks**. Collect all the old recipes from both sides of the family into a very **personal cookbook** for the newlyweds. Or gather recipes and household hints from close friends, and bind them in a special book, perhaps with a photograph of the couple on the cover.

For sushi devotees, consider a set of silver-tipped **ivory resin chopsticks** from Christofle ($42 a pair, 800-411-6515). You can send along a **sushi kit** with a bamboo mat, nori sheets, rice, fresh and pickled ginger, sesame shake, tamari, and organic vegetables such as avocados, carrots, green onion, and cucumber ($38, including FedEx delivery, Diamond Organics, 888-ORGANIC).

If the bridal couple likes to entertain, have **paper cocktail or luncheon napkins** printed with their monogram or name. Your local printing shop can handle this job, and it is surprisingly inexpensive. **Cloth cocktail napkins** are even better, and there are some very special ones at vintage stores.

The newlyweds will appreciate a **gift for the garden** if they're homeowners. I love giving plants because, if properly selected and cared for, they will grow along with the marriage for many years. For an autumn wedding, choose a **collection of daffodils** for naturalizing, and provide the manpower to get them in the ground. (Call White Flower Farm, 800-503-9624, or Dutch Gardens, 800-818-3861). Come spring, and every spring thereafter, the garden will fill with blooms as a reminder of the wedding and your gift.

A spring wedding could be the inspiration for an **orchard of fruit trees**, which will be in bloom each year on the couple's anniversary. Local nurseries will have the best idea of what to plant. Or you can orchestrate a **romantic rose garden**, filled with fragrant antique roses. Call Heirloom Old Garden Roses in Oregon (503-538-1576).

Another approach is to select a **large, beautiful vase** and send over

Gifts for Travelers

* **Books**. People who travel for pleasure often enjoy the armchair aspect of the trip as much as the actual journey; consult with your local bookseller for the latest in guidebooks and travel literature pertaining to their favorite areas.

* One book in particular—**a good atlas**, like the *Hammond New Century World Atlas* ($29.95).

* And while he's at home reading about his next adventure, he can brew a cup of tea in **a stunning turquoise teapot covered with a map of the world** ($45, Dandelion, 888-548-1968).

* **A subscription to a travel magazine**, such as *Travel and Leisure* (800-888-8728) or *European Travel & Life* (800-627-7660). Roll up and gift wrap a copy, using a map for paper.

* **A picnic for the plane**. In her ground-breaking book, *Chez Panisse Menu Cookbook* (Random House, 1982), famed chef Alice Waters describes one she made for a friend returning to Nice: " . . . roasted red peppers in olive oil, garnished with chopped garlic and sweet basil; young radishes and sweet carrots from the garden, as well as a tub of sweet butter; small pieces of leftover roast pigeon with rocket lettuces; tiny olives and goat cheese in a marinade with thyme branches; hard-cooked eggs; a dry sausage with cornichons and mustard; a few madeleines and some beautifully ripe and juicy nectarines and cherries." Imagine pulling out such a feast while your fellow travelers are dining on rubber chicken! If this sounds too tough to manage, you can buy an assortment of sushi for the in-flight enjoyment of the departing travelers (have them ask the flight attendant to refrigerate until mealtime) or maybe some nice cheese, fruit, and French bread.

* **A Frequent Traveler Case** with room for tickets, traveler's checks, currency, a passport, a pocket for your boarding pass, and a detachable day wallet, so you can leave your important documents at the hotel ($59.95, Levenger, 800-544-0880).

* **Auto Bingo** (four different kinds, $1.25 each at Dandelion, 888-548-1968).

- ✳ **Engraved brass luggage tags** with leather buckled strap (set of three, $18.50, Orvis, 800-541-3541).
- ✳ **A voltage converter**.
- ✳ **A prepaid phone card**.
- ✳ **A gift basket with their destination as the theme**: If they are going to Italy, include a bottle of wine, Frances Mayes' latest book about Tuscany, and an Italian phrase book.
- ✳ **Braun Travel Clock**, with light, snooze alarm, and world time zones ($42, Dandelion, 888-548-1968).
- ✳ **A journal**.
- ✳ Traveler's nightshirt for her, white cotton pique knit ($39, Chambers, 800-334-9790).
- ✳ **A silver plate travel shaving brush** ($40, Dandelion, 888-548-1968).
- ✳ The **Euro Interpreter**—a phrase translator, currency converter, and pocket calculator ($50, Norm Thompson, 800-547-1160).
- ✳ **A little tin of traveling tea**—green, black, or herbal (eight bags, $4.25, Dandelion, 888-548-1968).
- ✳ **A travel umbrella**, small and stormproof ($25, Travelsmith, 800-995-7010).
- ✳ **Traveler's writing chest**. Nineteenth century travelers were expected to return from their journeys with copious illustrated journals. If you'd like to see that charming custom revived, give this chest that contains a wooden pen with brass nib, spare nibs, a glass writing stylus, a bottle of black ink, and note paper. ($45, Lilliput Motor Company, Ltd., 800-TIN-TOYS).
- ✳ **Ready-to-Go Travel Kit**, including bottles for shampoo, conditioner, lotion, and pills; a mirror; deodorant, mouthwash, dental floss, toothbrush; razor, comb, scissors; nail clippers, tweezers; cleansing wipes, bandages; and a sewing kit ($65, Orvis, 800-541-3541).
- ✳ **A good map of their destination**. Call the Map Finder Service at Travelsmith (800-995-7010); if they don't have it, they'll find it for you.
- ✳ **Vintage luggage labels** from around the world, packed in a facsimile of an antique suitcase ($10, Dandelion, 888-548-1968).
- ✳ **A travel pillow** ($18, Travelsmith, 800-995-7010).
- ✳ **Single-use camera**.

several perennials and bulbs to be planted in a **Wedding Garden**, especially for cut flowers. Long-stemmed, fragrant Oriental lilies like Casa Blanca would be a good choice.

As the young marriage grows and flourishes, so, too, will the traditions that bind it together. You can help the couple foster such traditions in their marriage by starting a **collection of Christmas ornaments** for them. The hand-blown glass ornaments from Christopher Radko are especially collectible. This could solve your future gift-giving dilemma, as you can add to their collection annually.

A practical and remarkably cheerful gift is a **stockpot** or **set of soup bowls** from Williams-Sonoma or Crate and Barrel, paired with a **cookbook** or **your favorite soup recipes**, handwritten on index cards.

The Second Time Around

If the bride and groom have been married previously, have lived together before the wedding, or are a little older, they may already have a well-equipped household, so you can think of something more decorative or whimsical to give them. Gifts for a second or third wedding need not be as lavish as for the first, but they should definitely be given, along with your best wishes. You can send a pair of **crystal flutes and a bottle of good champagne** to their honeymoon destination. Another stylish gift for a mature couple is a **coffee table art book**; good sources for these include the Rizzoli bookstores and museum shops. **Monogrammed linens** are a thoughtful idea, particularly if the bride is taking a new name.

A romantic gift is a **hammock for two**. One of the best in the world is handwoven on Pawley's Island, South Carolina, and available at Hammacher Schlemmer ($110, 800-543-3366), or you can find beautiful and less expensive ones from the Yucatán peninsula.

Anniversaries

A wedding anniversary is the celebration of the endurance of a marriage, just as the wedding ceremony celebrates its beginning. Whether you mark the occasion with family and friends, or just the two of you, find a private moment for a review of your years together, and a quiet renewal of your commitment. If you can manage it, there is nothing like a brief, **romantic getaway** to remind you of why you got together in the first place.

In the early years of marriage, couples celebrating an anniversary may be given things to help them furnish their household, much like wedding presents. Parents or friends may want to take them out to dinner, but typically it is an occasion for a private and romantic celebration for two. If the couple saved the top of their wedding cake, they can share it on their first anniversary. Gifts to each other can be chosen by and for the two of them, such as **massage oil, pocket binoculars**, a **weekend away**, a **kitchen remodel**; or the couple can give each other **jewelry**. They may also create their own tradition of buying a **piece of furniture** or a **major household item** together. There are traditional gifts for each year of marriage (listed at the end of this chapter), and by following the custom, you can bring more significance to your choice of gifts. You could heed the French tradition, in which wives are often given a **rosebush** by their husbands on their anniversary, to symbolize their long-lasting love.

Couples celebrating their first through tenth anniversaries may want to consider starting some unique and fun traditions of their own. **Plan a trip each year** to somewhere sunny and warm. **Begin collecting** furniture for your home—even if all you can afford is a seat cushion. Make a **hope chest time capsule**. Each year on your anniversary, record your plans, hopes, resolutions, and dreams for the coming year, and open it on the next anniversary. This helps you keep track of your life and love.

Write each other an "I'm so glad I married you" letter, listing all the reasons he or she makes you sing with joy.

Save up all year and **splurge at the best restaurant** in town, and let that be the special place you return to year after year. My husband and I celebrated our first anniversary at Chez Panisse, with our one-month-old baby along. I'll never forget our waitress, who saw that our son was fussing and carried him around for an hour and a half while she poured wine and served food, and we enjoyed a private moment. We've returned every year since then.

A considerate gift to give a couple celebrating their anniversary is an **offer to take their kids**, to pave the way for them to go out for the evening or get away for the weekend. Send them on their way with a bottle of champagne.

Bake a second wedding cake for a favorite couple celebrating an anniversary. It doesn't have to be elaborate; frost it with white icing and top with a kitschy, plastic dime-store bride and groom.

The milestone anniversaries—tenth, twenty-fifth, and fiftieth— often include a gathering of the couple's friends, children, and family. **Make a video** of the whole gang and present it to the folks; it'll be a sensation at future family gatherings.

By the time a couple celebrates their twenty-fifth anniversary, the children have often left home, so an appropriate gift is to arrange for a **conference call** to tie together everyone in the family. If old 8mm home movies exist, you can transfer them onto a **video** and copy it for all the family members to view on the anniversary. Even if everyone cannot be together, you can still share in the memories.

Another way to capture the group for posterity is to go in advance to a **paint-your-own-ceramics** studio and buy a large platter with a supply of glazes. Have each family member decorate the piece with a signature or a drawing, handprints for the little ones. Then have the piece fired and send it to the celebrants.

Make a **patchwork quilt** or **anniversary tablecloth** with hand-prints, signatures, and decorations provided by the whole family.

Even if you don't usually give your parents a gift for their anniversary, the fiftieth anniversary is such a landmark that it should not be overlooked. There is no better time to gather for a **family reunion**, and if you can manage to collect your clan for an extended period, be sure to have plenty of film and easy-to-use cameras available for everyone. Take the film to a fast photo finisher, and while the group is still together, assemble the best shots in an **album** to give as a gift to the anniversary couple.

Present the anniversary couple with a **sketch or painting of themselves**, created by a talented family member or a professional artist. If your family happens to have artistic yearnings—and a sense of humor—have every family member draw their own version of the couple. Then bind the finished pieces together with the name(s) of the artist and a caption describing each one. It's great fun to compare the results!

You can also consider sending your parents on a **second or third honeymoon**: a cruise, a return visit to a place that holds romantic memories for them, or a trip to somewhere they always meant to visit. You can **send champagne to their room**, or arrange to have delivered to their table a food with special romantic significance to them, like **Baked Alaska**.

Send a note to friends of the anniversary couple asking them to remember the occasion with a **card** or **phone call**, relating special events from the past, memories, photos, or stories of a shared time. You can ask for this information in written form and assemble it into a scrapbook.

Because the fiftieth anniversary is traditionally celebrated with a gift of gold, you can give a **collection of antique golden roses** for their garden, perhaps one bush for each decade of marriage. *Graham Thomas*, *Symphony*, *Golden Wings*, and *Morning Has Broken* are beautiful, fragrant choices. Order from Heirloom Old Garden Roses, 503-538-1576.

A **garden bench with a brass plaque** is a good gift for one of the important anniversaries. If the couple has no garden, you might arrange to have the bench placed in a nearby park. (Wood Classics, 914-255-7871, has a wide range of benches, as well as plaques.) Or you can arrange to **plant a tree**, or a grove of trees, in their name in a spot that is special to them, whether it be their own garden, the campus of their alma mater, or a park they visit often.

The White House will send **greetings from the President** to couples celebrating fifty years or more of marriage. Make your request four to six weeks in advance by writing to: White House, Greetings Office, Room 39, Washington DC, 20502, or sending a fax to 202-395-1232.

Materials of Matrimony— A Year-by-Year Guide

First—Paper
A book of love poems, a magazine subscription, monogrammed stationery, concert tickets, a photo album filled with pictures of your first year together, a subscription to the Sunday *New York Times*, **plane tickets** to a romantic place.

Second—Cotton
Fluffy white terry robes for both of you, **flannel or cotton jersey sheets, thick bath sheets** (oversized bath towels), **a cotton cashmere blanket, an antique quilt.**

Third—Leather
A **leather chair, a lamb suede shirt, sheepskin slippers, sheepskin car seat covers, leather gearshift knob,** an **old leather-bound book, luggage, leather gardening gloves, desk accessories, belt, wallet, watchband, key chain, a baseball.**

Fourth—Fruit, Flowers
A **collection of antique roses** for your garden, **a fruit tree** (especially nice if it is flowering or fruiting on the anniversary), **fruit-of-the-month club membership.**

Fifth—Wood
A **picture frame with a photo of the two of you** (plus any kids, dogs, and cats you may have acquired), **a breakfast or dining table, a tree** you can plant together in the garden, **wood-handled cutlery, a wooden spoon, golf tees, a new deck, a humidor, a wooden hairbrush, a pair of Adirondack chairs** or **a teak bench** for the garden, **a cord of wood.**

Sixth—Candy, Iron
A **big box of their favorite sweets** (or you can **try making caramels or English toffee), fireplace tools, an iron bed, a clothes iron, iron barbells, a sword, a horseshoe, a garden gate, Japanese iron teapot.**

Seventh—Wool, copper, brass
A **wool blanket, a Shetland sweater, a cashmere robe, a copper weathervane, a copper pot, a copper pepper mill, a penny collection, brass tacks, brass candlesticks.**

Eighth—Bronze, pottery
Personalized door knocker, candlesticks, lamps, mixing bowls, canisters, a cookie jar.

Ninth—Pottery, willow
French or Italian **ceramic tableware** (platter, pitcher, vase, teapot), a **willow picnic basket** filled with favorite foods, **willow garden furniture**, a **weeping willow tree**, a **video** of the film *Willow*.

Tenth—Tin, aluminum
An **old tintype**, a **new fishing pole**, aluminum garden furniture, a **tennis racket**.

Eleventh—Steel
A **new car, stainless steel cutlery, eleven nail clippers, a Laguiole knife** from France.

Twelfth—Silk, linen
Silk or linen sheets, silk or linen pajamas, silk lingerie, silk boxers, a **silk-filled comforter.**

Thirteenth—Lace
Lingerie, of course. What else? **Lace curtains, lace handkerchief, Queen Anne's lace** (flowers), **shoelaces** (if your mate has a sense of humor).

Fourteenth—Ivory
Since the real thing is no longer politically correct or even legal, substitute faux ivory. **French flatware or serving utensils with "ivory" handles** are your best bet.

Fifteenth—Crystal
A **crystal-faced watch, crystal wine glasses, crystal salt cellars, quartz rock crystal**, a **crystal gazing ball**, a **crystal growing kit**, a **crystal radio.**

Sixteenth—Topaz

If you don't want to give jewelry, think of something this color, such as **clothing** or a **vase**.

Seventeenth—Amethyst

Earrings or **cuff links**, a **bouquet of violets, seventeen giant purple helium-filled balloons.**

Eighteenth—Garnet

Lingerie in garnet-red, a **garnet-red Porsche**.

Nineteenth—Aquamarine

A **swimming pool**, a **trip to the aquarium**, a **cruise to a Caribbean island**.

Twentieth—China

This is a good time to **begin a collection** if you haven't or replace any missing or broken pieces from the wedding set. Other ideas: a **china cabinet** or a **china cleaning service**.

Twenty-fifth—Silver

A set of **sterling silver flatware, silver tea set, silver jewelry**, a copy of **your wedding invitation engraved in silver**.

Thirtieth—Pearl

For her, a **pearl necklace** is always in style, or **pearl earrings**, for him, a **pearl tie tack** or for both, **dinner at an oyster bar**, in search of the real thing.

Thirty-fifth—Coral

A **trip to the Great Barrier Reef** (you can always buy a coral necklace when you get there).

Fortieth—Ruby

Forty ruby-red grapefruits, a **case of Merlot**.

Forty-fifth—Sapphire
The sky is sapphire blue and the sky's the limit—treat your sweetie to a **fabulous night on the town.**

Fiftieth—Gold
Matching anniversary bands.

Fifty-fifth—Emerald
A **trip to Ireland, a new lawn, an extravagant golfing trip or a visit to a rain forest.**

Sixtieth—Diamond
A **visit to a baseball diamond, diamond earrings, a diamond pinkie ring.**

Seventy-fifth—Platinum
When a couple has made it this far, they deserve to sit back and relax while family and friends plan the celebration. Perhaps a **platinum plaque** from Tiffany's announcing the momentous occasion?

3

Housewarming

The tradition of housewarming dates back several hundred years and must have originated as a means for the community to equip as well as celebrate new householders. We continue this practice today—when friends move in together, get a new apartment, or buy a new or first home. Whether or not there is a celebration, we like to mark the occasion with a gift.

Welcome Traditions

There is a tradition in Italy of giving a small plaque, called a **First Stone**, as a housewarming gift to ensure prosperity and harmony. The thick, rustic, handmade tile features a single image—an angel, a lemon, a bunch of grapes, a cornucopia—and although originally intended to be imbedded in the wall of the new house, it can be hung or used as a trivet ($30 and up, Niebaum-Coppola Estate Winery in the Napa Valley, 707-968-1135).

A traditional Jewish housewarming involves the hanging of a **mezuzah**, with a party following. There are several door mezuzah cases, ranging in price from $20 to $85 in the catalog called *The Source* *for Everything Jewish* (800-426-2567). In addition to the mezuzah, customary gifts of **candles, bread,** and **salt** are bestowed, to symbolize light, joy, and plentiful food in the new home. What could be a more appropriate wish, regardless of the religious persuasion of the new occupants? I love this gift for its simplicity and strength.

Fresh flowers are always appropriate to celebrate a friend's move to a new home or apartment, or even dorm room. But give the person a chance to unpack before delivering them or your gesture may be lost in the chaos of moving. Although I love the extravagance of fresh flowers, you might consider a **dried floral arrangement** or **wreath**, which will last practically forever. Shop at a local florist, or call Calyx and Corolla (800-800-7788) or 1-800-FLOWERS.

The Hungry Movers

Food of all descriptions will be received with gratitude in the midst of moving chaos, because less time spent preparing food is more time available for settling in. Take a **basket filled with the makings for an easy-to-fix pasta dinner:** fresh or dried pasta, sauce, a baguette, and a bottle of wine with some checkered napkins is a good choice. Or send something festive that can be offered to visitors who stop in, such as the **Venetian Wine Cake** or one of the **gift baskets** from the incomparable Balducci's of Greenwich Village (800-BALDUCCI).

Stonewall Kitchens (800-207-JAMS) has a catalog filled with jam, mustard, herbal vinegar, vinaigrette, infused oil, and sauces, all beautifully packaged for gift presentation. You can choose a single jar of **Blackberry Curd** ($6.75), the **Garlic Harvest Collection** ($21.95)—which includes the indescribably delicious Roasted Garlic and Onion Jam—or select a **gift box of three jams** ($23.95): Wild Maine Blueberry, Raspberry Peach Champagne, and Grand Marnier Cranberry Marmalade. You can be sure that anything you choose from this company will be delectable and perfectly presented.

Give the busy movers an excuse for a mid-morning break: assemble a **basket full of brunch goodies,** including croissants and bagels, smoked salmon, cream cheese and jam, good coffee, fresh orange juice, and a couple of colorful napkins, and deliver it along with an offer to unpack boxes or move furniture.

Baskets from Manhattan Fruitier look more like still life paintings than produce and make an exquisite gift ($50 and up, 800-841-5718). This is the gift basket to send if money is no object and you really want to impress. They may be filled with only fruit or may contain your choice of comestibles: biscotti, cheese sticks, chocolates, and cheddar cheese. The baskets themselves are beautiful, and the presentation is sublime.

A **Brunch Basket** ($53, Miss Grace Lemon Cake Co., 800-FOR CAKE) could be a welcome arrival when the moving van leaves. It includes a willow serving tray with three minicakes (lemon, California orange, and chocolate fudge), plus a banana pecan chocolate chip loaf and gourmet coffee.

A cookie jar filled with homemade cookies spells relief for anyone involved in the rigors of moving. Shop for a humorous old cookie jar at an antique store, or fill a large canning jar, and deliver it with a **pound of coffee beans**, maybe the House Blend?

For a more substantial feed, Clambakes-To-Go (800-423-4038) will send out a **full clambake feast**, with forty-eight hours notice. Live lobsters, soft shell steamer clams, mussels, corn on the cob, potatoes, onions, and Italian link sausage come packed with fresh seaweed in their own steamer pot, with lobster claw crackers, seafood forks, lobster bibs, and wet naps on the side. All you need to do is add water or wine, or both. Even if your friends haven't unpacked the kitchen yet, they can dine in style ($136 for two, FedEx overnight delivery included).

Wine is a great housewarming gift, whether it be a bottle, a pair of one red and one white, or a mixed case with all sorts of choices. You can shop locally, call my favorite wine purveyor, Mill Valley Market Wine Shop (800-699-4634), or shop on line at the Virtual Vineyard (www.virtualvineyard.com).

Learning the Ropes

Moving to a new community, or even relocating across town, can be intimidating. Your dwelling is turned upside down and all the familiar landmarks change. Settling in involves not only unpacking all of your

More Gifts for the Garden, Deck, Porch, and Patio

* Snow shovel
* Birdhouse
* Birdseed and a bird feeder
* Mailbox
* Wind chimes
* Retractable clothes line and wooden clothes pins
* Rain gauge
* Volleyball set
* Thermometer
* Doormat
* Telescope and star-gazing book
* A charcoal or gas grill
* A hammock
* Croquet set
* A portable outdoor fireplace
* A garden bench
* A terra-cotta pot filled with colorful annuals
* A single fruit tree or an orchard
* An antique rose collection

worldly possessions, but also finding your way in a new neighborhood. One of the most thoughtful housewarming gifts I've heard of was given to a friend by a man who had lived in her new town for his entire life. He compiled a **book of top local recommendations**: which dry cleaner to use, restaurants to frequent and avoid, the friendliest gas station in the world—all the things you need to know when you move to a new place and usually spend months finding out. Then he invited her over for a **casual cocktail party** to meet the neighbors. What a welcome!

If you have a new neighbor arriving from outside your area, **collect maps and brochures on local points of interest** and present them along with a **subscription to a local newspaper**, or a **gift certificate to a local restaurant or store.**

For families with children, the **welcome book** could also include suggestions for reliable baby-sitters, kid-friendly restaurants, information on Girl Scouts and Little League, and an invitation for a play date to get the kids acquainted. Parents with children moving to a new community will be anxious about their kids, so anything you can do to help them settle in will truly be a thoughtful gift.

When you pay a call to welcome a new neighbor, bring along a **wreath** for the front door. There are wreaths appropriate for all seasons of the year; it is no longer only a Christmas custom.

On the Practical Side

Here's a gift your friends will thank you for eternally: arrange for a **cleaning service** to come to their old house or apartment on moving day. Heaven knows it's hard enough to move without having to deal with the dirty work of cleaning up the old place, and this will enable them to get on with the really fun part of unloading boxes at the new residence. If the new abode is in a shambles, send the cleaning service there instead. Or you can hire a **window washer** to do the new place, inside and out, before your friends move in. Even if the house has been cleaned before moving day, chances are the windows have not, and it makes a huge difference.

You can **volunteer to set up housekeeping**: arrange closets, settle the new kitchen, organize the book shelves, but only if you are known for your legendary organizational skills. Otherwise, give the gift of a few hours' **consultation with a professional personal organizer** who is equipped to handle these all-important details.

People who are moving from an apartment into their first house need all kinds of things that you can give as housewarming gifts: a **ladder**, a **vacuum cleaner**, a **spade and fork**, **books on gardening**, a **hose**, **tools for simple carpentry and plumbing chores**, a **grill and barbecue accessories**, a **cord of wood**, a **fireplace screen and tools**. If your budget is slim, give them a **cookbook**, **fireplace matches**, a **supply of light bulbs**, a **rechargeable screwdriver**, **hot pads and dishtowels**, a good **broom and dustpan**, a sturdy **flashlight**, or a **perennial plant for the garden**. Fill a wastebasket or bucket with **cleaning supplies**, or wrap a collection of **refrigerator magnets** in a **checkered dish towel**.

Put together an **emergency-preparedness kit**. Contents will vary depending upon the region of the country and disasters that may be encountered—power failures, flooding, freezing, earthquakes, and so forth—but most should contain a flashlight, a water supply and iodine tablets to make safe drinking water, candles, some canned goods. A **home first-aid kit** can be included in the above, or given as a gift in itself.

Home Pages

Any good bookstore will have a large variety of books related to homes and home maintenance. **A Mr. Fixit–type book** is an important addition to the library of any new homeowner and will be a long-lasting and oft-thumbed reminder of your thoughtfulness. *The Pocket Idiot's Guide to Trouble-Free Home Repair* by David J. Tenenbaum ($9.95) has instructions on how to change washers in leaky faucets, fix faulty wiring, and find studs for picture hanging. *The Stanley Complete Step-by-Step Book of Home Repair and Improvement* by James A. Hufnagel ($25, Simon & Schuster) will teach you all this and more with 2,000 full-color step-by-step instructions.

When you visit friends in their new home, give them a **guest book** and be the first to sign it. Any journal or blank book will do nicely.

Gifts from the Grocery

* **Jams**

* **Olive oil**

* **An assortment of teas**

* **Unusual candy**

* **Every hot sauce you can find**

* **Smoked salmon**

* **Caviar**

* **Special honey**

* **Collection of ice cream toppings**

* Buy **a pumpkin or coconut**, write the name and address of the gift recipient on it, and send through the mail, no wrapping required.

* **A sampling of microbrewery beers**

* **A case of assorted wines**

* **Popcorn, seasonings, and a bowl**

The charming book *Home*, edited by Sharon Sloan Fiffer and Steve Fiffer ($12, Pantheon), is a collection of essays and memories that proceeds one room at a time, from "The Bathroom," by Jane Smiley, to "Garden," by Bailey White. It is a heartfelt housewarming gift, especially for someone making a home for the first time.

For your style-conscious friends looking for inspiration for their new digs, consider giving a subscription to the British magazine, *World of Interiors* (0044 1858 435 359), or the French magazine, *Cote Sud* (www.condenast.com).

If the new house has a garden, give your friends a **book on garden design**, or **growing vegetables**, and include a **selection of seeds** or a few **six-packs of annuals**.

A friend of mine was losing her beloved neighbor who was about to move after twelve years of living next door. Before the moving date, she took a portrait of herself with her neighbor, standing in front of the house. She chronicled the move, photographing the backyard where their children had grown together, the boxes being packed, the moving truck loading up, then driving away. She assembled the photographs in a small **album** and presented them to her friend when she visited her in her new home.

If you have a friend who is moving out of town, assemble a **gift box with stationery**, a **roll of stamps**, and a **promise to write**.

Thoughtful Touches

A **gift certificate to a local home/hardware/garden store** or a **home furnishings chain** like Pottery Barn (800-922-5507), Home Depot, or IKEA (800-434-4532) is perfect, even for the person who has everything. You can put the gift certificate inside a Lincoln Log or Lego house.

A housewarming gift suitable for anyone, whether they've just moved into a mansion or a studio apartment, is the **Ultimate Dust Pan** from Restoration Hardware (800-762-1005). It is a triumph of industrial design—simple, elegant, and functional. No one should be without one, so buy one for yourself while you're at it; only $16.

Another treasure from Restoration Hardware is the **Original Russ-**

ian **Flashlight**, powered by human energy. If you've ever reached for a flashlight only to find the batteries dead, you'll understand the beauty of this. Squeeze it, and it always works. Forever. The funky Russian packaging alone makes it worth the $10 sticker price.

If you know the style of the new house and the taste of the new owners, beautiful **house numbers** are a gift they'll always remember. It's sometimes hard to find nice ones; Restoration Hardware has several to choose from in brass and iron, as well as **personalized house plaques** with the family name and address. Lillian Vernon also has a wide assortment (800-285-5555), and is always a good value.

I love oversized **coco fiber welcome mats**. Their generous dimensions make the entryway more grand and cut down on tracked-in dirt. Frontgate (800-626-6488) has this hard-to-find item in several sizes, including 48 by 30 inches, $55, and 72 by 36 inches, $95.

A **skein of raffia** looks great hanging on the wall of a new kitchen or in the entryway on the coat rack; the strands of raffia are eminently useful for tying up packages, plants, and old newspapers ($16.50, Langenbach, 800-362-4490).

The Great Outdoors

Sometimes it's preferable to give a gift for outside the house, rather than inside, particularly if you are unsure of the person's taste or decorating style. One beautiful idea is a collection of **daffodil bulbs for naturalizing** in the garden or grounds (White Flower Farm, 800-503-9624). "Naturalizing" simply means that you plant them and forget about them. If conditions are right, blooms will appear annually and multiply over the years. It's easy—plant the bulbs in the fall, they'll put on a show in the spring. You could be a really good friend and provide the bulbs as well as the manpower to get them in the ground.

If you're invited to a housewarming party, you might consider pooling your resources with other guests to give a significant gift. Several friends might want to join together to give a **commercial outdoor heater**. This is a rather extravagant housewarming gift to be sure, and really more accurately a patio warmer than a house warmer. The first time I saw one was at an outdoor restaurant on San Francisco Bay. It was a beautiful, starry night, but too chilly to consider dining al fresco. Wrong! This terrific device allows you to enjoy the outdoors, even when the temperature dips. It is substantial, 7'8" high, and delivers enough radiant heat to warm an area 8' by 12'. Call Hammacher Schlemmer (800-543-3366) for more details.

4

It's a Boy, It's a Girl!

These days, we call them "baby showers," but the tradition of gift-giving on the joyous occasion of a birth goes back to a time long ago when women first joined together to see that a new mother was given the knowledge and equipment she would need for the birth and care of her newborn. In Victorian England, this task was the duty of the vicar's wife, who sewed baby clothes for the deserving poor of the parish. Today, many mothers-to-be have already bought the basic layette, and your gift might be of a more fanciful nature. Find out if the baby you're shopping for is already equipped with the necessities, then go from there. Newborn basics include **diapers** and **diaper bag**, **undershirts**, **pajamas**, **hats**, a **basket**, **cradle** or **crib** and **bedding**, **car seat**, and **stroller**. Be sure to ask the new mom for suggestions—she may have clear ideas about what she wants and needs.

Start Something

If you are a godparent, grandparent, or other close relative of the baby in question, or if you are just a good friend who plans to stay in touch, you can choose a birth present that will be the beginning of a lifelong collection. This is the kind of gift that will become more meaningful to the child as time passes. It can be a **coin collection**, starting with a proof set of coins from the baby's birth year. Or consider starting a **string of pearls** for a baby girl by giving her an **Add-a-Pearl necklace**. You'll find these at fine jewelry stores, where you'll make the initial purchase of a delicate gold chain and one, three, or more tiny pearls, depending on your budget. You can add more pearls on subsequent birthdays, and the necklace looks sweet no matter how many pearls are on it.

Or you can give her a ½" sterling silver **birthstone ring** on a sterling silver chain, to be worn when she's a little older (ring, $20; chain, $12, Signals, 800-669-9696).

Another gift for a baby girl is a **beautiful dollhouse**, to which you can add furnishings on future gift-giving occasions. There is a good two-story wooden dollhouse in the Hearthsong catalog (800-325-2502) for $99. This is one of those gifts she'll have to grow into, but what a wonderful thing to look forward to!

You can start a **library**, beginning with classics like *Pat the Bunny*, *Goodnight Moon*, and *The Little Fur Family*, and progressing to more "grown-up" books each year. Combine a great book with a little animal: *Make Way for Ducklings* **with a rubber ducky**, or *Blueberries for Sal* **with a stuffed bear**. This is an especially fitting gift to be given by an older sibling or cousin who can remember favorites. Or give a **book on infant massage** (Babies love it!) with **a bottle of unscented sweet almond oil**.

Don't overlook the idea of starting something in the financial realm: a **travel nest egg**, **college trust fund**, or a **stock portfolio**. The parents will certainly be grateful, and so will the child, when the time comes.

Treasured Keepsakes

When you want today's gift to become tomorrow's heirloom, the incomparable Tiffany's (800-526-0649) is tough to top. Their signature blue box proclaims an occasion of import, and the contents never disappoint. Choose one of their **baby rattles** ($60–130), the classic looped **feeding spoon** ($95), **a cup** ($180), **square picture frame**

($145), **comb** ($85), or **natural bristle brush** ($300), all in sterling silver and suitable for engraving. If the baby's name and birth date are not yet determined, you can purchase the gifts and return them later for monogramming. Tiffany's also has an engraved **sterling silver birth record frame** ($285). To encourage fiscal responsibility at an early age, consider a hand-painted earthenware **bunny bank** with a tiny gold key, available in pink or blue ($60).

If you enjoy spending time looking around antique and collectible shops, you can find terrific one-of-a-kind baby gifts that are instant heirlooms. Possible discoveries include **christening gowns, silver spoons, antique toys,** a **rocking horse, child's chair** or **wagon, patchwork crib quilts, antique frames** for all those baby pictures, and **embroidered baby pillowcases.** You may find a **ceramic divided dish** with a hot water reservoir for warming baby food, or a **tiny silver box** that could be earmarked to hold baby's first curl.

Start a **collection of the classics** (see book list on page 67).

For a **personalized birth book** mom and baby will love, consider *Special Delivery* from Create-a-Book ($11.95, 800-598-1044). This thirty-five-page illustrated storybook will be interwoven with the name of your special baby and a lot of details, including parents, hometown, doctor or midwife, date and time of birth, weight, and size. The book even mentions baby's first visitors.

Be the one who remembers to buy a **newspaper** on the birth date, in the baby's hometown. It is a thoughtful and personal gift, and one that the new parents may just be too busy to remember until it's too late. You can also **videotape the news of the day,** or buy a handful of **magazines from the week of the birth.** All this will be endlessly fascinating to the child as she grows.

If you're a photographer, give the parents a **gift certificate for a photo shoot,** to be redeemed some time in the first year. My very favorite baby photo is a black-and-white portrait taken by a photographer friend of one of my sons at six months, playing with the lawn sprinkler.

Another heirloom of the future: the **Baby Time Capsule** from the Original Time Capsule Company ($19.95 plus shipping, 800-729-8463), which includes the book, *What It Was Like the Year You Were Born,* six pieces of "letters to the future" stationery, and special sealing labels and instructions.

Parents can start a **treasure box** for the newborn and add to it throughout childhood. Include in it lullabies the baby listened to, a favorite blankie, the first pair of shoes, the books that were read again and again, and photographs. Each object can be labeled to explain its significance in the child's life. An appropriate time to present this gift might be when the child reaches adulthood at eighteen or twenty-one.

Ever wonder where you can go to **get baby shoes bronzed** these days? Send $30 for one shoe or $50 for the pair to Exposures, 800-222-4947, and they'll send you a certificate to be redeemed for the all-metal antique bronzing of baby's first shoes or sneakers, along with a pre-addressed shipping bag.

Crib and Carriage Accoutrements

The single most indispensable article of newborn baby gear just might be the **Lamby**, a short-shorn, natural lambskin imported from Australia. Babies seem to settle in more easily when lying atop this cozy skin, whether it is in the crib, the stroller, the car seat, or on the lawn. They are used in neonatal units of hospitals throughout the country, where a greater weight gain is reported for babies using the sheepskin. The Lamby absorbs moisture, so baby stays warm in winter and cool in summer, and of course, it is machine washable. Order directly from the importer, Lamby Nursery Collection (800-669-0527).

Garnet Hill (800-622-6216) was the first company in the United States to import flannel sheets from England, almost twenty-five years ago. They're still at it, and they now have a full range of **flannel bedding for baby**, including **sheets, pillowcases, and comforter covers** in solids, stripes, and adorable prints, like Stars and Clouds and Hats and Shoes. You'll also find **quilts** ($75) and a hard-to-find crib-size, waterproof **flannel mattress pad** ($28). There are soft, simple woven **cotton baby blankets** in pastel colors ($42) and a **hand-hooked wool rug** ($195) featuring the three bears, marching with bowls of porridge in their paws.

You can have a soft, knit **personalized baby blanket** with the baby's name, birth date, time of birth, and birth weight, along with a personal message, by calling the Canadian company, Blankees (888-BLANKEE).

Blankets are available in receiving ($22.50) or crib size ($35.25), and several colors and styles. My favorite has a border of hearts across the top, and teddies in the bottom corners. Blankets are acrylic but can be ordered in cotton or wool for an additional charge.

A sweet, old-fashioned idea for a baby gift is to make a **friendship quilt**. Get together six, nine, or twelve of the mother's friends and relatives, and ask each to contribute a quilted square. You can follow a theme, or let the quilters choose their own direction. The best seamstress in the group can volunteer to sew the squares together with a filling and backing. After the baby has graduated to a bigger bed, the well-worn quilt will end up on the wall as a treasured memory.

Babies sometimes feel more secure sleeping with a **night-light**. Moms and dads love them too, as they guide the way to their baby's room at night and just generally look cheery. There are many on the market, inexpensive and indispensable.

Even if you're not very handy, you can make a **wreath to hang over baby's crib**. Start with a simple base of grapevine or straw, and use ribbon to tie on a collection of tiny animals (a menagerie of eight is available for $9.95 from Hearthsong, 800-325-2502). The baby will look at it and point, eventually learn to say the names of all the animals, and probably remember the wreath forever. When the child is old enough, the ribbons can be untied and the animals added to the toy collection.

When it's time for a stroll, baby can step out in style in the **Classic English Perambulator** made in England by Silver Cross, since 1877. This luxury carriage has a zinc-coated steel frame, a hand-finished body, and hand-painted pinstripes on the cover, as well as a soft-ride suspension and those terrific-looking, oversized wheels. You can practically picture Mary Poppins at the helm, with her young charge in control. At 66 pounds, it's not exactly portable, but you can't have everything. Available for around $1,000 from Hammacher Schlemmer (800-543-3366).

Baby Clothes

When choosing baby clothing, you needn't stay with newborn sizes. If the mother has a lot of friends, the baby may acquire more snappy outfits than he can possibly wear before he moves on to the next size, especially if he has older siblings who are passing on their favorites. So, you might consider the six month, nine month or even one year size, and calculate how old the baby will be at that time, so you can avoid buying a sunsuit that will fit her in mid-January.

If you live near a Gap Kids or Baby Gap store, your dilemma is over. Picture Junior in **denim overalls** ($24) or **khakis** (with a snap crotch, of course, $19.50) with a **polo shirt** ($12.50), or a classic Gap **white pocket tee-shirt** ($6.50) peeking out at the collar. A **baseball cap** ($10.50) and **argyle socks** ($3.50) complete the picture. Take one of their **minisize jean jackets** to a sewing shop to have the baby's name embroidered on the back.

Equally alluring fashions can be found for baby girls at Baby Gap. It is so much fun to mix and match in this store that before you leave you'll wish you had more little ones to buy for, or maybe even one of your own! If Junior already has overalls, no problem—merchandise can be exchanged at any Gap throughout the country, which offers a distinct advantage over shopping at a local department store, especially if your gift is going to an out-of-town recipient. (Call 800-333-7899, ext. 72344, for the store nearest you.)

Hanna Anderson (800-222-0544) is one of the best options if you prefer the convenience of shopping by mail. They're famous for their **striped long john jammies**, in great colors such as fuchsia and pink, royal blue and green, and navy and gray. There is a version for newborns called **Zippers and Stripes** ($30), adapted for easy diaper changing. Their tie-on **Pilot Caps** ($8) in solids and prints are as cute as they are practical. Hanna clothes are made of fine Swedish cotton and are so well constructed that they never wear out. If you send back your outgrown clothes, you'll receive a 20 percent credit, and they'll pass on the "Hannadowns" to needy kids. Another great gift is Hanna's **"Everything-But-the-Baby" Bag** ($58), a roomy, modern-day diaper bag of a sturdy black fabric made from recycled plastic with the look and feel of cotton, and a built-in changing pad that snaps down or zips off. This is a diaper bag that's not too feminine for Dad to feel comfortable carrying.

If you want an even more **fashionable diaper bag**, Barney's has one from Kate Spade with a roll-up mat—Mom or Dad will feel very smart while changing the little one ($200, 212-826-8900).

For a little something that's inexpensive but fun, wrap up a stack of **colorful bandannas**, essential gear for teething time starting at about six months. You'll find these for under $2 at most variety stores.

A place to hang all those adorable hats and clothes: the **Eames Hang It All** by Herman Miller, available through the Museum of Modern Art catalog ($45, 800-793-3167). Brightly colored and ever-so-stylish, this clothes rack is as useful as it is fun.

Gifts from the Garden

If you want something unusual for a spring baby, consider giving a **Birth Tree**. Consult with your local nurseryman to find a tree that will be in bloom at the time of the birth, and every year thereafter on the birthday of the child. Some particularly beautiful choices include dogwood, flowering cherry, and crabapple. Decorate the tree with little gifts like a **silver spoon**, a **silver dollar from the birth year**, or an **assortment of booties**. Plan a tree-planting ceremony with the parents and new baby, and take a birthday photograph each year to chronicle the growth of the child and the birth tree together. You can shop at a local tree nursery, or call Sonoma Antique Apples, 707-433-6420.

There is an old custom in the Jewish faith to honor a newborn by planting a tree—cypress for girls, cedar for boys—which traditionally was used to make the chuppah or wedding canopy when the child grew up. Now, you can **have a tree planted in Israel** in honor of a baby's birth, and a certificate will be sent to the parents. For details, call the New York office of the Jewish National Fund (212-879-9300).

A collection of antique roses is a beautiful garden gift for a summer baby. Classic roses are worth seeking out, because although most bloom only once a year, the plants live longer, are often very fragrant, and are easier to grow than the more widely available hybrid tea roses. To give the collection special meaning, choose from varieties with names such as "Baby Love," "Breath of Life," "Angel Face," and, "Happy Child." To order, call Heirloom Old Garden Roses, 503-538-1576.

More Gifts for Baby

* Sheepskin moccasins

* Zipper jogging stroller

* Crib mobile

* Kelty baby backpack

* Astrological reading

* Personalized scrapbook

* Ultra Heart and Sound Soother

* A teddy bear dressed in a baby cap and fun socks

* Baby monitor

Special Delivery

A thoughtful little catalog, largely undiscovered, is *A Child's Dream* (800-359-2906), filled with products made from natural materials. Especially for the newborn you'll find **Rose-Colored Glasses for Baby** ($22), which are really two yards of rose-colored china silk to drape over the cradle and bathe the baby in a soft light. Dreamy.

Another little-known children's catalog is *Animal Town* (800-445-8642), dedicated to cooperative learning. For baby, consider the **rag doll mouse, bunny,** or **bear** ($24)—cuddly felt dolls dressed in colorful floral and checked clothing that is easy to remove. It's not hard to imagine one of these becoming a favorite throughout childhood.

Gift Baskets

Filling a gift basket is a great way to give a lot of little gifts and create a feeling of abundance. Come up with a theme, and use your imagination.

To make a **baby bath gift basket**, start with a plastic baby tub and fill it with a **baby towel**, a **natural sea sponge**, some special **soap, shampoo,** and **powder** just for baby's sensitive skin (I like the natural products from Weleda). You can get an outstanding, **oversized hooded towel** in 9 ounce (super-heavy) terry for $23 from Pinwheels, a small mail-order company in Seattle, 206-488-0949. Be sure to include a supply of Tub Tea's **Herbal Brew for Baby's Bath**, oversized tea bags filled with calendula, chamomile, and lavender, to cleanse and soothe baby's sensitive skin (three bags, $12, available at Restoration Hardware, 800-762-1005). And don't forget the **rubber ducky.**

The Body Shop (800-BODYSHOP) offers a ready-made **mother and baby gift set** ($22), which includes **Baby Bath, Baby Shampoo, Baby Lotion, Baby Bottom** (a nonpetroleum-based barrier cream), and **Nurturing Cream** (for pregnant and breast-feeding mothers), packed in a handy tote.

For **baby goes to the beach**, start with a **bucket**, and fill it with **sunglasses, baby sunscreen,** a **wide-brimmed hat**, a **sun suit**, an inflatable **beach ball**, and a **beach towel.**

The **bedtime baby basket** could include a **crib pillow, pajamas,** a night-light, a **hot water bottle** to warm the crib, a **teddy bear**, a copy of *Goodnight Moon*, and a **tape or CD of lullabies** (I love Linda Ronstadt's *Dedicated to the One I Love,* or you can order a *Personalized Disney Lullabies Tape* in which six familiar lullabies are sung using the baby's name, available from The Lighter Side, 941-747-2356), all loaded into a **wicker laundry basket.**

Gifts for Mommy and Daddy

In the excitement of a new birth, the baby will usually get an abundance of attention, but sometimes the parents are the ones who need a little coddling. Dads, epecially, often feel left out. So if someone you know becomes a new father, think about giving a gift to him, instead of his baby. It could be a **pound of coffee**, or a **case of wine**, with a note saying, "Believe me, you'll need this!" Or get him a **"Mr. New Dad" tee-shirt**, which shows dad diapering the dog while baby drinks out of the dog bowl (The Lighter Side, 941-747-2356). The tone and the gift depend on your relationship, but your thoughtfulness will be appreciated.

When you go to visit the new baby in its first days, take along a **birthday cake**, decorated with flowers and ribbons. The parents will enjoy celebrating, and they'll have something special to offer the baby's first visitors.

All mothers need pampering, but never more so than following childbirth. I love the French custom in which the new mother's father and her husband both give her **flowers**.

It is difficult for a new mom to take much time away from her baby, so you can **offer to care for the little one** while she takes advantage of your gift: a **manicure and pedicure**, a **massage, hot tub,** or **facial**.

A new father can show his love for his wife and his awe at the miracle of birth by giving her a **locket** to hold the baby's picture, and, later, a first curl. I can't imagine any new mother who wouldn't treasure such a gift. It's also a lovely way to signify the child's first birthday, since the birth of a child, especially a first or only child, changes a woman forever in a way that nothing else will.

You can contribute to the new library of **parenting books** they will, no doubt, be collecting, especially if you have some can't-live-without titles based on personal experience.

The Healthy Baby Meal Planner by Annabel Karmel makes a great gift, paired with a **Happy Baby Grinder**, an inexpensive and indispensable little gizmo that turns practically anything into the consistency of baby food. Parents will be well-equipped when baby starts eating solid foods in the months to come.

For something a little more irreverent, but deeply moving, no new parent should miss *Operating Instructions* by Anne Lamott. A chronicle of the author's first year with her son, it'll make great reading for a nursing mom, or a dad up pacing with the baby at 3 A.M.

If you're short on cash and long on time, or just want to proffer a really helpful gift, give a **book of baby-sitting coupons** to the new parents.

They will also appreciate help with **housecleaning**. You can arrange a visit from a service, or, if that's too pricey, assemble your own bucket and cleaning equipment and roll up your sleeves.

One thing new parents agree upon is that infants generate an astonishing volume of laundry, especially given how tiny they are. The gift of a **laundry service**, yours or a professional, will help out in the early days.

To give them more time to be with their baby, and to sleep, offer to **bring over a dinner**. A catered dinner on the first night home can be the occasion for a quiet celebration. If you don't cook, or haven't got time, order from a **local food delivery service** or go in with a group and have meals delivered once a week for the first month. This gift is a universal favorite among new parents. One friend's mom signed her up for a month's worth of dinners with a culinary service that made weekly deliveries of five entrees, with enough leftovers for lunches. Be sure to find out ahead of time which nights suit them best, and whether there are any dietary restrictions or preferences.

New parents get little time to themselves, so a **gift certificate for a dinner out** and an **offer to take care of the baby** while they're gone will be met with a sigh of thanks. It may be months before they're able to take you up on the offer, but they'll love it.

A friend recently visited her brother and sister-in-law, who had just become parents of twins. Her gift to them was four days of her undivided attention to the family. She cooked and baked, did laundry, and got up for the babies' twice nightly feedings. After four days of being pampered, the sleep-deprived parents felt human again, and my friend took away with her the memory of two little faces she'll never forget.

Gifts for Siblings

If there is an older brother or sister, it is considerate to give a small gift to this little person who may be a bit put out by all the attention lavished on the new arrival. Even if you just bring a **little toy** or a new **book,** the parents will appreciate your peace-keeping gesture.

The older child may have just been forced to abdicate his special position as Baby of the House. You can give a gift that will honor the new, more grown-up status; a **big kid pillow,** or a **small backpack** to help carry baby's things (Lillian Vernon, 800-285-5555, has several for under $10). You could also give him a **bottle** just for him to feed the baby with.

If the baby will be sharing quarters with an older sibling, your gift can be something for their room, like a **poster,** a **night-light,** or a **growth chart.**

Make a special date with the older child for the two of you to go out and have fun together, if the two of you are close. Mom will be grateful for the break, and the child will be happy to get away for a while.

5

I Love You!

The roots of our modern Valentine's Day lie in the ancient Roman fertility rite of Lupercalia, a Roman feast dedicated to the pastoral god, Lupercus, and the goddess of love, Venus. As part of the ceremony, the names of Roman maidens were placed in one urn and those of the young men in another, then names were drawn in a matchmaking ritual.

February 14 is also associated with the martyrdom of Saint Valentine, who is now known as the patron saint of lovers everywhere. He was put to death circa A.D. 269 for performing secret marriage ceremonies in defiance of the Roman Emperor Claudius II. This day is also held by Europeans to be the day birds pick their mates.

Through the centuries, this day has been celebrated in many different ways throughout the Western world. In medieval England, girls believed they would marry the first boy they saw on Valentine's Day. Similarly, those struck in the heart by an arrow from the bow of Cupid, the Roman god of love, would fall in love with the next person they looked at. Italians met in the garden to listen to poetry and music. Name drawing much like in ancient Rome became an English practice:

boys and girls drew from a box the names of members of the opposite sex, and the two were then said to be valentines for the coming
year.

Valentine's Day is the one official day of the year to celebrate love,
but you can find opportunities every day to show your affection, and
your gesture means even more when it's unexpected.

Romantic Expressions

Today, we celebrate Valentine's Day by expressing our love, romantic or platonic, to sweethearts, family, and friends. **Hearts and flowers,
candy,** and **poetry,** the good old-fashioned ways of saying, "I love
you," are still the best.

The sending of **love poems** and messages first became a custom in
1416 when the Duke of Orleans sent love poems to his wife while he
was held captive in the Tower of London. This evolved until the custom of **handmade valentines** reached its zenith in the late 1800s, and
today, many Victorian valentines are now considered works of art.
Even now, despite all the beautiful greeting cards on the market, nothing surpasses a handmade red, white, and pink confection of ribbons
and lace, cutout hearts, and doilies, with a sweet sentiment inscribed. If
you have taken the time to make a card your gesture is, in itself, an
expression of love, and the esthetic outcome of your creative efforts is
almost incidental.

Another idea for a homemade valentine is to construct a large envelope from beautiful, handmade paper, perhaps one that contains dried
flower petals. Trim the envelope with lace and fill it with red, white, and
pink buttons and confetti, hearts cut from felt, and whimsical gold
charms. You can insert a giant decorated, heart-shaped cookie or a
scroll of paper with a love poem written on it. If this doesn't touch the
object of your affections, nothing will!

Love Letters

Kate's Paperie (800-809-9880), in New York, has more than 5,000
different papers on which to write your love notes. An **Italian glass**

dipping pen, scented inks from France, and stationery trimmed
with laser-cut 19th-century Belgian lace designs will put you in the
mood for amorous eloquence. Or you can send writing materials to
your loved one, done up in Kate's incomparable gift wrap, and sit back
and wait to receive your own romantic missives. Kate's also offers the
instructive tome, *How to Write Love Letters*, by Michelle Lovric
(Shooting Star Press), which you may want to buy for yourself or send
to someone as a subtle hint.

Add more than a touch of mystery with **disappearing ink**—it turns
blue when paper is warmed (Fountain Pen Hospital in New York, 212-
964-0580).

If you've written a love poem you want to immortalize, you can have
it, or anything for that matter, silk-screened onto chocolate (Richart
Design and Chocolate, 800-RICHART). Or leave the poetry to a pro:
Give your valentine a copy of *The Love Poems of John Keats: In
Praise of Beauty*, written for his beloved Fanny Brawne. Or for him:
Elizabeth Barrett Browning's *Sonnets from the Portuguese*, penned for
her husband, Robert. Or choose *In Their Own Voices: A Century of
Recorded Poetry*. This four-CD set of 122 pieces represents every
major poet of the twentieth century, including Whitman, Yeats, and
Maya Angelou ($59.98, Signals, 800-669-9696). Read to your love from
a beautifully illustrated version of Pablo Neruda's *Twenty Love Poems
and a Song of Despair* ($12.95, Chronicle Books), *Diaries of a Young
Poet* by Rainer Maria Rilke ($27.50, W. W. Norton), or a volume of
Shakespeare's sonnets.

Don't forget to write your own **love notes signed by "A Secret
Admirer."** Disguise your handwriting and send one to your spouse,
then watch his quizzical look as he tries to figure out who sent it.

Express Yourself

Western Union (800-325-6000) is still alive and well; you can send a
hand-delivered telegram expressing a sweet sentiment (one to fifteen
words, $17.95, plus $13.95 for in-person delivery). Or perhaps a
singing telegram will give you just the edge you need; these are delivered via telephone by Western Union.

A slightly different twist is **Send-a-Song** (about $9.95, 800-SEND-

More "I Love You" Gifts

*   **Bubblebath**

*   **Picture frame** to hold a romantic photo of the two of you.

*   **An evening of dancing**

*   **Silk boxers**

*   **A museum visit**

*   **Picnic basket** filled with strawberries, chocolate truffles, red wine, and a book of love poems.

*   **Eros Tea** from Mariage Freres (The Gardener, 510-548-4545).

A-SONG). You specify the date and time, they'll place the call to your sweetheart and play your personalized message, then the song of your choice, which you'll select from their vast collection. Maybe "Let's Spend the Night Together" by the Rolling Stones, or "You Are the Sunshine of My Life" by Stevie Wonder? Or, perhaps, vintage Sinatra. Request your special song, and let it be from an anonymous amore.

If you're feeling a little more flamboyant (and flush), consider **skywriting** (around $850 for eight characters, look in the Yellow Pages under Aerial Advertising). You can tell your sweet to be on the lookout, and when "I Love You!" puffs across the sky, lovers all over town can imagine the message is meant for them. A somewhat more affordable, and only slightly less romantic, approach is an **aerial banner** (about $250 for up to forty characters), which has the added advantage that it can be saved for posterity.

If all this sounds too lofty, be a little more down to earth. Get a **giant banner** proclaiming your undying love, and put it up for all the world to see. You've heard about these on the news, now you can make the news! Order the banner from Supergram ($9.95, 800-3-BANNER). It's up to you to figure out how and where to hang it, but if the freeway seems a little too public, stretch it across your driveway or wrap it around the house.

Sports fans: arrange to **have your romantic message posted on the scoreboard**, then lure your sweetheart to the game with a pair of tickets. (Call the specific venue for information.)

H a v e   a   H e a r t

One of the most romantic couples I know gives an **annual valentine's party** and has a friend take a few casual photos of each couple attending. The film goes to a speedy processor, and the best shot of each couple is put in an inexpensive frame and sent off with a note about how nice it was to have them over. If the party's on Saturday, guests receive the **valentine photos** by the following Tuesday. They're thrilled, and many of the people report that it's the first photo taken of the two of them in years.

The same friends give annual gifts on Valentine's Day, rather than at Christmastime; they've adopted Valentine's Day as their holiday of choice. "Heart" is the operative word: **graduated heart cookie cutters**, a **heart-shaped baguette** (talk to your local bakery), **heart ice-cube trays** (Lillian Vernon, 800-285-5555), **heart-shaped Angel vine topiary** ($20, By The Vine, 888-298-4384, or on-line at www.bythevine.com), **heart baking pans** (Williams-Sonoma, 800-541-2233), **heart lollipop cookie molds** (Sur La Table, 800-243-0852), **note pads with hearts**, a **heart-shaped cutting board** (The Bowl Mill, in Weston, Vermont, 802-824-6219), **heart-shaped pasta** (Buckeye Beans & Herbs, 800-449-2121), a **personalized, heart-shaped brass door knocker** (Lillian Vernon, 800-285-5555), or **heart confetti**. For a tiny token of your affection, get a **rose quartz heart** (1½", $3.50 from A Child's Dream, 800-359-2906), or get several and give a little treasure to everyone you love. Many of these are available only around Valentine's Day, so it's a good time to stock up on tokens of affection you can give throughout the year.

Sew Romantic

Even if you're not much of a seamstress, you can make **valentine pillows** for everyone you love; they'll think of you every time they cuddle up. Cut out two heart shapes of soft or sexy fabric—silk, velvet, satin, or fleece—stitch together, leave a little opening, then fill with lavender blossoms and buckwheat hulls, available in bulk at natural foods stores.

You can do this sewing project on a smaller scale: Cut out two 2-inch red felt hearts, sew them together by hand with matching or contrasting embroidery thread, fill with stuffing to make a **puffy heart**, and finish sewing shut. Glue a pin to the back and voilà! Valentine jewelry.

Love in Bloom

Flowers are a traditional expression on this romantic day. The classic choices are **long-stemmed red roses**, but don't let that stop you if you'd rather give **peonies** or **snapdragons**. Personally, I prefer roses in all the soft, sorbet colors: peach, cream, salmon, and white. Choose a reliable mail-order or on-line source for flowers, including 1-800-FLOWERS and Calyx and Corolla (800-800-7788), or shop at your local florist, where you can see exactly what you are getting. You can use the language of flowers to communicate your feelings by choosing blooms that speak your mind: roses signify love, but yellow roses mean jealousy; red rosebuds stand for purity and loveliness, daisies mean innocence; lily-of-the-valley means a return of happiness; violets stand for faithfulness; rosemary is for remembrance; and forget-me-not speaks for itself.

For Valentine's Day, 1-800-FLOWERS has dozens of possibilities for flowers with a heart theme: the extravagant **Heart of Hearts** ($125), a huge heart constructed of roses and freesias in shades of pink, purple, lavender, and white, which lies on the table as a center-piece and then dries beautifully; and several more modest choices, including a **heart-shaped wreath** made of grapevine and decorated with dried flowers ($45).

If your sweetheart is a gardener, by Valentine's Day she will already be poring over seed catalogs and planning what to plant in the coming spring. Give her a **fragrant, antique red rose plant**, or put together a **collection of romantic roses** like "Belle Amour," "Kiss of Desire," "Gentle Touch," and "Sweet Dream." You can order these for about $11 each from Heirloom Old Garden Roses in Oregon (503-538-1576), where they have a friendly horticulturist on staff to help you with your selection. In most parts of the country, February is too early to actually put anything into the ground, so they'll send it at the appropriate time for planting in your area. You can snip photographs from their catalog, and give it to her along with a bouquet to let her know what's coming.

Sweets for My Sweet

Say it with flowers in a whole new way, with **flower ice cream**. Out of a Flower, Inc. (800-743-4696) makes forty-five flavors of ice cream and sorbet from edible flowers and fresh herbs, with all natural ingre-dients and no preservatives. They are sold at 125 stores, including Dean & Deluca (call 800-221-7714) and Whole Foods Markets (over 100 stores nationwide, check their website at www.wholefoods.com for the location nearest you). They will also pack the ice cream in dry ice and ship it all over the country (there is a five-pint minimum), and yes, it arrives frozen solid. It is pricey, but very special. Their sorbet flavors include: Rose Geranium Blossoms, Red Rose Blossoms, and Passion Fruit with Red Rose Petals. Talk about romantic!

Another flowery idea is the **Romance Gift Box** ($26 from Le Cordon Bleu, 800-457-CHEF), which contains Rose Buds Tea and Rose Petal Preserves from France.

Valentine's Day and chocolate go hand-in-hand. La Maison du Chocolat (212-744-7117), the Parisian chocolatier, offers some of the best chocolate in the world. Their New York store will send out their signature brown box filled with anywhere from 2 to 215 delectable **French confections** of your choosing, or you can call the legendary Leonidas (212-980-2608) and put together your own assortment of **Belgian pralines, white coffee creams**, and **truffles**. And, if that doesn't sound special enough, call on Teuscher Chocolates of Switzerland (800-554-0924) deemed by many connoisseurs to be the world's finest. Their house specialty is **champagne truffles**, a blend of fresh cream, butter, and chocolate with a champagne cream center, dusted with confectioner's sugar. This is also the place to go for the classic **red heart box filled with chocolates**, which will make anyone feel like a movie star from the forties.

Send your chocolate lover a heart-shaped **truffle cake** ($27.50, from Miss Grace Lemon Cake Co., 800-FOR CAKE), or a signature gold foil **ballotin filled with fine chocolates** from Godiva Chocolatier (order on-line at www.godiva.com, visit one of their 150 boutiques nationwide, or call 800-9-GODIVA).

Remember the little puzzles you had as a child, where the object was to get the little silver balls into the indentations? Now there is an edible version of this: a **valentine puzzle** of Swiss milk chocolate with four little white chocolate hearts decorating the corners, and cinnamon red hots to roll into the shape of a heart. All this fun for only $5 (Dandelion, 888-548-1968).

Recipes for Romance

There is an old saying, "Food equals love." What better way to show your love than to **prepare a special meal**—remember the film *Like Water for Chocolate*? If you're all thumbs in the kitchen, or haven't the time, **hire a caterer to fix dinner for the two of you**. Call a culinary

Gifts for the Chocoholic

* **A 5-pound Hershey's milk chocolate bar** ($49.95, Hershey's, 800-454-7737), which looks just like the smaller version and measures 18" x 9".
* **Chocolate Band-Aids** "for life's little boo-boo's" (box of ten Choc-Aids $4, at Daily 2-3-5, a quirky Greenwich Village shop, 212-334-9728).
* **Camp Chocolate**—A boxed set of six campfire memories, including a canoe with two seats, a kerosene lantern with a red flame, and a yellow-and-white fried egg "sizzling" in a frying pan, all rendered in milk, dark, and white chocolate ($15, Whispering Pines, a catalog for the cabin, 800-836-4662).
* **Basket of Chocolate Treats**, filled with twelve different chocolate goodies, including cappuccino white chocolate chunk cookies and toffee nut malt balls ($59, 1-800-FLOWERS).
* **A Williecake**, the world's richest, densest, darkest chocolatiest chocolate torte ($32, 911 Gifts, www.911gifts.com).
* **Homemade chocolate-chip cookies**.
* **A pint of chocolate ice cream** in a cooler packed with dry ice.
* **Sneak-Peak Candy Sampler** ($4.95, 714-496-3851) is a little gizmo that will allow the chocoholic to take a core sample of the bon-bon from the bottom to avoid detection. Brilliant.

academy in your area to ask about engaging a student who may be more enthusiastic and less expensive than an established firm.

You can plan a stay-at-home Valentine's Day and **rent a romantic film classic**, like *Doctor Zhivago, Casablanca,* or *Gone with the Wind,* make some buttered popcorn, and light a fire. If you're busy people and you go out all the time, this could be the best way to celebrate. And if she's crazy about black licorice or Peanut M&M's, have a supply on hand.

If you want something a little more substantial, Clambakes-To-Go (800-423-4038) will send out the full **clambake feast for two** (see page 58) with forty-eight hours' notice.

For a more **elegant candlelit supper**, you can dine on oysters and champagne and **hire a string quartet** to play for the two of you. Call the high school, college, or university music department near you to arrange for the musicians.

Champagne and Caviar

Champagne and caviar signal a special occasion and will never go out of style. There is a certain elitism surrounding their consumption, but there is really only one thing you need to remember: Buy the best you can afford. A few of my favorite champagnes are Veuve Clicquot and Roederer, but for a lower priced, domestic sparkling white in the champenois tradition, Mumm's Cuvée Brût or Sharffenberger are good bets. Wrap up your favorite bottle with a copy of ***Champagne—The Spirit of Celebration*** by Sara Slavin and Karl Petzke ($22.95, Chronicle Books).

Be sure to buy your caviar from a reputable supplier who sells enough of the stuff to keep the stock fresh, rotated, and properly stored. Petrossian (212-245-0303), the fabled importer of Russian caviar, will send you Beluga, Ossetra, or Sevruga in several sizes from 30 grams to one kilo. They also have imaginative gift ideas, like the **New York Hat Box** with 125 grams of Sevruga caviar, a large tin of chocolates, smoked salmon, goose fois gras with truffles, and blinis; or their version of a sample pack called **The Five Muses** ($177), which contains 30 grams each of Beluga, Ossetra, Sevruga, and pressed caviar, as well as salmon roe. Nice. This is also the source for the requisite **crystal service and gold and silver serving utensils**, the use of which will surely enhance your enjoyment of fine caviar. Another great source is Caviarteria (800-4-CAVIAR), which offers most of the above and more, including a selection of nine different **caviar spoons**, all made of English ram's horn or mother-of-pearl ($8–75). They also offer same-day delivery, if you're caught in a "caviar emergency." If you tend to procrastinate, this is worth knowing about.

Mood Enhancers

Follow your champagne and caviar with a **romantic bath for two**; float rose petals in the tub, or soak in an herbal brew made with the **Romance Blend** from Tub Tea (three bags $12). These sachets are oversized tea bags filled with flowers and herbs (available at Restoration Hardware, call 800-762-1005 for the store nearest you). Or prepare a **Milk Bath with Roses** ($4.50, from Renaissance Spa Treatments, 800-406-BATH).

Wrap up a stack of **romantic CDs**. Some of my favorites include: *The Best of Chet Baker Sings*, k.d. Lang's *Ingenue, Heartstrings* by Earl Klugh, *Aretha Franklin Sings the Blues*, Miles Davis's *Sketches of Spain*, John Coltrane's *1962 Ballads*, Anita Baker's *Rapture*, Ravel's trios and sonatas, Rachmaninoff's Second Symphony, Debussy's *La Mer*, and *Amore: The Great Italian Love Arias*.

If you love someone who loves to play games, get him or her a personalized **board game starring the two of you**, with hand-drawn artwork and trivia questions. Call Anyone's Game, 800-448-5431 ($110, including shipping). One romantic young man arranged to have his **marriage proposal hidden in the solution of the *New York Times* crossword puzzle**, then made sure his girlfriend did the puzzle. Although it is unlikely that the *Times* will print your proposal, you may be able to involve your local paper in a little romantic collusion.

Too tame? Check out the catalog from Good Vibrations, 800-289-8423, or visit one of their sex-toy stores in San Francisco or Berkeley. Some of the most popular gift items: *Herotica*, a book written for women from a woman's point of view, the **Hitachi Magic Wand Vibrator** ($45), and the best-selling *101 Nights of Great Romance*, sort of a sexually oriented how-to book/calendar. Other fun toys to choose from: **Tasty Tickles Body Powder, Midnight Fire edible** gel, and **two-foot long ostrich feathers** in a rainbow of colors. There is even a very sexy board game for couples called **Romantic Rendezvous**. Their telephone sales staff are trained sex educators, and they are discreet, friendly, and helpful.

She'll love **sexy, silky lingerie** for Valentine's Day, and so will he, so this is a gift that either party can bring to the other party. A good place to shop is Victoria's Secret—they have several stores, or you can call for their famous catalog, 800-888-1500; at least you'll have a great time thumbing through it.

Love On-line

There's a new store on the World Wide Web called 4 My Love, which specializes in romantic gifts for women. You'll find flowers, chocolates, and gifts, all with romance in mind. The **Rosebud Heart Wreath** ($69) is breathtaking and long lasting because the roses are dried. Individual **chocolate letters** ($21 for the set) can be used to spell out your edible, amorous message. Of course, if you can't decide between roses and chocolate, you can always kill two birds with one stone and get her **a trio of chocolate roses** ($14). Check out 4 My Love at www.4mylove.com.

Between the Sheets

What better occasion than Valentine's Day to give your sweetheart a set of luxurious sheets? Cotton is cool, linen is chic, and silk is sexy, but for coziness on those cold winter nights, nothing compares to flannel. Garnet Hill (800-622-6216) has been importing English cotton **flannel sheets** for over twenty years, and theirs are the best. Wrap up a bright red, vanilla-scented, **heart-shaped hot water bottle** with the bedding, and use it to warm up the bed before you get in (about $27 at Fillamento, the famed San Francisco housewares emporium, 415-931-2224). Better yet, make up the bed with fragrant **rose petals tucked between the sheets**.

For something a little more elegant, choose an embroidered **cashmere pillow sham** from the venerable Italian firm of Pratesi (800-332-6925). This is also the place for **His and Hers cashmere robes**. They may cost more than your mortgage, but I can't imagine anything more luxurious, unless it's the ankle-length **cashmere and silk robe** lined in silk charmeuse from Chambers ($750, 800-334-9790).

For the same luxury with a smaller price tag, what about a pair of stonewashed **silk charmeuse pillowcases** in pink for Valentine's Day? ($19 each at Chambers, 800-334-9790)

Here's to Healthy Hearts

The image of hearts used to conjure up one thing: romance. But in recent years, you might also think of preventing heart disease. The **American Heart Association** (888-889-0322) welcomes donations and has an annual promotion around Valentine's Day, so your valentine's gift could be **a contribution in the name of a loved one**. Other gifts to promote a healthy heart might include **membership to a gym**, a **cross-country ski trip**, a **cookbook full of healthy recipes**, or the latest in **at-home exercise equipment**. Or you can send a **Heart Healthy gift basket**, with no saturated fats, oils, or cholesterol, but a lot of fresh fruit, jam, honey, tea, crackers, and sparkling cider ($35 and up, Sandler's Gift Baskets, 800-75-FRUIT).

Getting away from It All

The **minivacation** is a great way to renew bonds and rekindle romantic feelings. Jet away to some secluded spot for a long weekend, have a fling in the city, or spend the night in a nearby bed & breakfast; every region of the country has its own great B&B guide, so check your local bookstore. Plan whatever you can fit into your schedule and budget. It's even more exciting if you can keep it a surprise. You can even conspire with your partner's office mates to try to carve out a few unscheduled days. Tell your traveling companion only what to pack for—city, country, skiing, beach—but don't give away the destination, and don't forget the champagne! You could wrap up a map, tracing the route and highlighting the rendezvous location, to be opened en route. This is an especially great gift for men to give, because many seldom do this sort of planning. Hawaii and Mexico look pretty good in the dead of February, and air fare to Europe is drastically reduced at this time of year. How about **Valentine's Day in Paris**?

Gifts That Cost Nothing and Mean Everything

* **Call your parents on your birthday** to thank them for giving you the gift of life.
* **Put a note in your child's lunch box.**
* **Give someone a beautiful bouquet** from your garden.
* **Smile for no reason.**
* **Write a letter to a friend.**
* **Take your dog for a swim** on a hot summer day.
* **Pay or pass on a compliment.**
* **Give away something you love** to someone you love.
* **Send a tape of your current music picks** to an old friend you haven't seen in a long time to tell them about yourself through music rather than words.
* **Get a library card** for a young friend.
* **Make coupons:** "Good for . . . (massage, car wash, grocery shopping, carpool driving, baby-sitting, pet-sitting, plant-sitting, snow shoveling, lawn mowing, standing in line so that you don't have to)."
* **Use your bonus airline miles to send someone on a trip.**
* **Share your travel experiences on tape** (parents love this).

Jewels and Gems

A **special piece of jewelry** is a wonderful way to say, "I love you." Remember, it's the thought that counts. A trinket from a bubblegum machine or a Cracker Jack box can be just as prized as an expensive gem. I myself am partial to the **candy necklaces** available exclusively at this time of year.

You can shop locally at jewelers or antique stores, or call Tiffany's (800-526-0649). Any jewelry will do nicely, but for a valentine theme, choose from their **love knot earrings** ($200) or the **"Hearts" necklace** ($175) and **matching bracelet** ($90), all in sterling silver, or the **Crossed-Heart pendant** in 18k gold on an 18-inch chain ($400). If you're contemplating an engagement, but not quite ready to buy the ring, you can drop a broad hint with Tiffany's **"Diamond" paperweight** in full lead crystal ($105). While you're at it, ask for their free booklet on how to select an engagement ring.

A great on-line source is the Museum of Jewelry (www.museumof-jewelry.com). Their collections include museum reproductions from Greece and Rome, the Renaissance, and Victorian times, and most pieces are priced at under $100.

A sweet valentine gift especially for a young lady: a **necklace for her to string from fresh water pearls and rose buds** ($15, A Child's Dream, 800-359-2906). The Nature Company (800-227-1114) has a beautiful **amber heart necklace** on an 18-inch sterling silver chain, $19.95.

A **charm bracelet** is old-fashioned and romantic and will provide endless opportunities for gift giving as you add to her collection. Choose a romantic charm, or start a theme bracelet based on her interests: gardening, cooking, sports, travel.

A good old-fashioned silver **ID bracelet** used to signify "going steady," and it'll still warm the heart of any girlfriend, new or old. An **Irish Claddah ring** carries a lot of sentiment, too.

For a little **bauble in the four figures**, turn to Asprey (212-688-1811), best known for their rare stones and superb craftsmanship. A **calfskin jewelry case** from Asprey is a bit more affordable, starting at $145. Styled like a miniature suitcase, with a tiny lock and key, it comes in several great colors, including Asprey's signature purple.

Expressions of Love

Imagine walking out under the night sky with your inamorata and pointing up to a **star you have named in her honor**. It seems a bit presumptuous, sort of like selling the Brooklyn Bridge, but, still, there is a certain romance to it. For $45, The International Star Registry (800-282-3333) will handle all the details for you and send a parchment certificate identifying the telescopic coordinates, as well as a celestial chart with the star you named circled in red.

My favorite gift ever was a fluffy ball of real live **puppy**. **Kittens** and **bunnies** are also irresistible; just make sure in advance that the recipient is willing and able to have a long-term relationship with a pet.

Use your imagination to assemble a **Gift for the Five Senses**: something to please the eye, a fragrant gift, a present to please the ears, a taste treat, and something soft or tactile to appeal to the sense of touch. It could be as simple as a beautiful vase, perfume, a romantic CD, a box of chocolates, and a bottle of massage oil. Or more elaborate, such as a photograph of the two of you, a scented candle, tickets to the symphony, caviar, and a velvet scarf. For the sense of sound, you could choose a music box that plays "your song" (San Francisco Music Box Company, 800-227-2190).

Good Scents

A gift of **perfume** is very personal, and a little risky, but take a chance. When you choose a fragrance for someone, it is a signal that this is a scent you would like her to wear because it pleases or excites you. Therefore, you must approach the selection very carefully and not be unnecessarily swayed by the salesperson helping you. Her favorite fragrance, or mine, will not necessarily be yours, and if you don't make the decision, the gift loses its special meaning.

Bath powders and **oils, pillows filled with herbs**, **potpourri**, and **scented candles** are a nice way to give a fragrance if you're unsure about perfume. If you are a woman choosing a scent for a man, you should first determine whether or not he will wear a cologne; many men will not, and your gift will fall flat.

Mending Fences

If you've had a spat, sometimes a gift can open the door of communication again. The cleverest one I've heard of was as follows: a heartbroken but determined young man called up a well-known gardening company and said he wanted to order two things to have shipped to his girlfriend. First, he sent her a **kindling ax**, with no message included. Then, the next day, he sent her a **border spade** with the message, "Let's bury the hatchet—I love you!" I don't know what the poor girl thought when she received an ax in the mail, nor did I ever learn the outcome of this unusual gesture, but if nothing else, she got two great tools.

The traditional symbol of peacemaking is an **olive branch**, so if you can't find a real olive branch, you can take off from that idea and send a **jar of olives**, or a **plate with an olive pattern** on it, along with a conciliatory note. You'll find an 11" square glazed ceramic olive plate at Sur La Table ($19.95, 800-243-0852).

Love All Year Long

Valentine's Day is just the beginning of being romantic. It is the one day of the year when it is expected of you; all of the other days are opportunities for thoughts and gestures, large and small, that will let your loved ones know how much you care. Read Gregory J. P. Godek's *1001 Ways to Be Romantic*, and implement just a fraction of his suggestions, like toasting to each other every time you open a bottle of wine. Here's one of mine: Save some of the **candy conversation hearts** you can buy around Valentine's Day to put in your kids' lunch boxes, or hide in your mate's sock drawer, throughout the year.

Present your sweetheart with **a case of champagne** and tag each bottle with a date upon which the bottle is to be shared for a romantic evening.

On Valentine's Day, or any day, **leave a note or a balloon on the windshield** of your sweetie's car to get the morning off to a great start.

Send an e-mail or leave a voice-mail message just to say, "I love you."

If your love travels frequently, you can make sure he remembers you by sending a **little surprise to his hotel**. When he arrives, he'll be greeted by a **plate of your homemade cookies**, a **soothing CD**, or an **aromatherapy candle** (the Tangerine and Lavender blend will please him or her, $6.95–31.95, Illuminations, 800-CANDLES). Pick up your companion at the airport, instead of having him take the shuttle, and greet him with a bottle of champagne and a reason to celebrate: He's home.

6

Happy Holidays

December is filled with holidays. At the end of the year, many cultures and religions take time out from the busy work-a-day world to reconnect with their heritage. Whether it be Kwanzaa, remembering African roots; Hanukkah, recalling an ancient and miraculous victory; or Christmas, symbolizing the birth of Christ, each celebration holds light as a central theme. The winter solstice, which marks the return of the light, was the most important holiday of the pagan calendar. It seems that humans have forever had a basic need to affirm life at the darkest time of the year. Sometimes the commercialization of these holidays—especially Christmas—can be overwhelming. On the other hand, there is something truly wonderful about the opportunities they offer us for remembering our friends, appreciating our loved ones, and recognizing the joy, harmony, and hope that exist in the world.

Kwanzaa

Kwanzaa is a new holiday, created in 1966 by Dr. Maulana Karenga to give people of African descent an opportunity to reconnect with the past and reaffirm the heritage and culture of Africa. It means "first fruits" in Swahili and is based on African harvest festivals. The celebration begins on December 26 and lasts for seven days. Presents from parents to their children might be **gifts from Africa**, including dolls, drums, flutes, and other instruments, or **books about African heritage**. Other fitting gifts might be a *mkeka* **(straw mat)**; **fresh fruits and vegetables**; an **ear of corn** for every child in the family; a *kinara* **(candleholder)**; seven **black, red, and green candles**; or a **unity cup**—all of which are used symbolically in the Kwanzaa celebration. There is an excellent book called *The Gifts of Kwanzaa* by Synthia Saint James ($5.95), Albert Whitman and Co., which simply and colorfully explains this holiday to children.

Hanukkah

Hanukkah, the eight day Festival of Lights, is celebrated by Jewish people to remember the victory of the Maccabees over Antiochus more than two thousand years ago. On each of the eight nights, the menorah is lit with the family gathered around, and often the children of the household are given a gift. In American Jewish families, the presents are usually similar to what would be given at Christmas. This occasion can be used as a time to focus on being a family, and **family gifts** may be given instead of, or in addition to, small individual gifts. One night the family gift can be a **book**, which is read aloud, another night it can be a **board game** everyone will enjoy playing. There is also the tradition of spinning the **dreidel**; in the catalog called *The Source for Everything Jewish* (800-426-2567) you'll find over twenty different dreidels, including a sterling silver rendition ($55), and a two-foot dreidel pinata ($15) for a little cross-cultural fun.

This same aptly named catalog offers a stunning array of **menorahs**, **Hanukkah gift wrap**, **Hanukkah gelt** (gold-foil wrapped chocolate coins), and Hanukkah gifts for all ages, from newborn on up. It also features Kosher gourmet food, including a **Deluxe Lox Box** with bagels and dessert and a **Glatt Kosher salami gift assortment** with all the trimmings ($39.95 each). Or let the folks at E.A.T. (212-772-0022), Eli Zabar's Manhattan eatery, put together a sensational **holiday food basket** ($75-150) filled with Hanukkah treats including gelt, candles, and an edible menorah made of challah (Jewish egg bread).

Hershey's offers a few less traditional, but tasty alternatives: a **Happy Hanukkah Gold Gift Tin** tied with a big blue bow and filled with chocolate, and a **Happy Hanukkah Card** consisting of 2 pounds of solid milk chocolate embossed with a greeting and a menorah, which can be personalized with up to twenty-four characters ($16.96, 800-454-7737).

The Metropolitan Museum of Art (800-662-3397) is a good source for traditional Jewish gifts, including a **Kiddush cup** ($50), **Star of David and Menorah bookmarks** ($24), and a brass **paperweight** which says, "hava" ("love") in Hebrew ($65).

Christmas

The gift-giving tradition associated with Christmas may have its roots in the story of the Three Wise Men, who traveled to worship the infant Jesus bearing gifts of gold, frankincense, and myrrh. The spirit of Christmas and the modern-day Santa Claus also hearken back to St. Nicholas, a 3rd- or 4th-century humanitarian who cared for the poor, especially children. Obviously, this focus on children is still in force today, as can be quickly confirmed by asking any child which holiday is his or her favorite.

In my family, Christmas, more than any other holiday, is steeped in tradition. Each year on December 15 we decorate the biggest tree we can find. Fitting the tree into its cast-iron base is always a big production, and my husband tries to refrain from profanity as he wrestles with the tangled strings of colored lights. Boxes of ornaments are pulled out of the basement, with exclamations of recognition as each one is unwrapped from its protective tissue. It's like a reunion with old friends. Some were made by the children when they were younger: treasures of felt and clothespins, pine cones and glitter. The tree is always topped with the red and green God's Eye ornament woven of yarn and twigs by one of my oldest friends many years ago. Our first batch of Christmas cookies is baked beforehand and consumed with eggnog while the decorating proceeds. Christmas music is played for the first time. Each year, the tree-decorating ritual unfolds in just the same way. Even some of the gifts are a ritual, like my husband's annual gift of ten pounds of **pistachios**, wrapped in the same tassled foil box each year. It is these traditions that bind us together as a family and make Christmas feel like Christmas.

Helpful Holiday Hints

Let's face it: holiday gift buying can be a real headache. Like millions of others, I vow each year to complete my shopping before Thanksgiving, and like most of them, I fail annually. It's a wonderful idea to shop for this season throughout the year and stockpile gifts, but few of us actually pull it off. Fortunately, there are catalogs and stores galore that are more than happy to help us find the perfect gift for everyone on our list—right up to the last possible moment.

If you are a catalog shopper, you will receive a plethora of seasonal offerings in the months prior to the holidays. While you are casually browsing through them, tear out pages as gift ideas occur to you and file them away with the recipient's name noted. Hopefully by mid-November your file will be thick, and the mail-order houses will still have stock of the merchandise you want. Sit down with a cup of tea and a credit card, and get on with your shopping, unharried. Or, turn on your computer and stroll around the on-line virtual shopping malls, which include many of the same stores you'll find in the real mall.

Some people find it helpful to computerize their gift-giving with recipients' names, addresses, an accounting of what you've given them in the past, and what they've given you. If this works for you and helps you to relax at this hectic time of year, by all means do it. Personally, I prefer to be more spontaneous. Either way, a list of giftees is essential, a budget for each is helpful, and checking the names off as you match a gift to a person on your list is oh-so-satisfying. If you're out shopping, treat yourself to lunch, maybe a quick makeup lesson at the cosmetics counter, and the occasional gift for yourself. Have fun!

Limiting your shopping to one or two places, rather than going to every store in the mall, and every mall in town, will do wonders for your sanity. Restoration Hardware gets my vote for one-stop Christmas shopping. Here you'll find something useful, clever, and imaginative for nearly everyone on your list, and tons of unique stocking stuffers. You'll find gardening goodies, a thoughtful book selection, tin toys, furniture, lighting, and yes, hardware. You'll also find oddball and intriguing items, like a real, working **miniature cannon** and the world's best **ginger ale**. With seventy stores across the country, there'll probably be one near you. Call 800-762-1005 to find out.

A friend asked for holiday gift-giving advice from her venerable English aunt. She replied: "Do as I do. **Write checks and order pears.**" Everyone on her list receives one or the other, and Auntie is serene and confident while the rest of us are going crazy with our holiday shopping. This is certainly an approach worth considering.

Of course, it's nice to be personal and to choose a unique gift for everyone, but if you find something terrific, there's nothing wrong with buying it in multiples and giving it to several of the people on your list. Besides fruit, consider a **calendar**; **paperwhite narcissus, amaryllis,** or **other bulbs** for indoor forcing; a beautiful **wreath**; an annual **ornament**; or **smoked salmon**, a **food basket**, or a favorite new **cookbook**.

Low-Cost Treasures

A gift needn't cost money to be special. You can give a **gift certificate for a service: baby-sitting, dog-walking, lawn mowing**. One friend I know records a **cassette of music**, customized to fit the taste of the recipient. Then she creates a cover using a color photocopy, a drawing, or a photo. If you have an artistic talent—writing, drawing, painting, photography—you have a gift to give. Likewise, if you have a skill such as accounting, massage therapy, or carpentry, you can offer your services. The **gift of time** can be the most valuable one of all, since it's in such short supply these days.

My next door neighbor loves to bake and annually makes an outrageous array of **holiday cookies and candy**; then she and her children call on the neighbors, delivering the homemade goodies. It is a priceless, and yet inexpensive, gift. This old-fashioned gesture serves as a reminder of what the holiday is supposed to be about.

A Remembrance of Things Past

Remember those heavy **lead icicles** you hung on the Christmas tree as a child? Then, one year, the lead icicles were nowhere to be found. (Lead icicles were banned in the U.S. because of the danger of lead poisoning in children.) In their place were inferior aluminum wisps that stuck to your clothing when you passed the tree. They weren't heavy enough to hang properly, and they were no good for wadding up into hard little balls and throwing at your brother. Well, the lead icicles of your childhood are back, imported from Germany and only $2 a box, in a very special San Francisco store called Dandelion (888-548-1968). This store also features a tiny **hurdy-gurdy** that cranks out "Jingle Bells." The brass movement is fascinating to watch, and at $2.75 each, you can buy a handful of them and attach one to every gift you give. These are terrific finds; the cost is nominal, they make a great gift in themselves, and they turn an ordinary gift into something special.

Stocking Stuffers

My children say that opening stockings is their favorite part of Christmas. Each of them has a **big wool stocking** with his name knitted on the cuff (available for $40 from Garnet Hill, 800-622-6216), and every year on Christmas Eve, when the fire has died down to embers, we read *A Visit from Saint Nicholas* and hang our stockings from the mantel. We still leave cookies for Santa and a token carrot for the reindeer. The next morning, the cookies are gone, the carrot nibbled, and sooty hoofprints lead away from the hearth. The stockings are filled with Christmas candy, a piece of fruit in the toe, and a lot of fun little things collected over several months. Good old-fashioned Christmas candy is hard to find these days, but one place to look is Williams-Sonoma (800-541-2233), which features **Hammond's Art Candy** ($17)—those handmade confections with Christmas images that run through the whole piece—and enormous **striped lollipops** right out of my childhood.

Other great stocking stuffers include the following:

* Slinky
* A colorful, **hardwood spinning top** ($5.95, A Child's Dream, 800-359-2906)
* **Sidewalk chalk,** six bright colors and two white sticks ($1.95, Hearthsong, 800-325-2502)
* A tiny, **hand-hammered copper bell** ($15.50, A Child's Dream, 800-359-2906)
* A **red velveteen bag filled with twenty-five magnets** ($12.95, Hearthsong, 800-325-2502)
* **A hacky sack** ($6, Chinaberry Books, 800-776-2242)
* **Card games:** Children's Authors, Women's Authors, Inventors, Shakespeare ($5 each, Dandelion, 888-548-1968)
* A **tin of French paper clips** ($5, Kate's Paperie, 800-809-9880)
* **A special coin purse** with a bill tucked inside
* **Godiva's mocha cinnamon coffee beans**
* **Matchbox cars**, for kids of all ages
* **Tiny Lego sets**
* **A small bottle of French perfume**
* **A Santa Pez dispenser**
* **Chocolate coins**
* **A Swatch watch**
* **Carmex lip balm**
* **Pop-up sponges**
* **A single-use camera**
* **Refrigerator magnets**
* **Travel-size toiletries and toothpaste**
* **A hot water bottle**
* **Monogrammed luggage tags**
* **Rubber stamps and colorful stamp pads**
* **Jacks**
* **Blank audio- and videotapes**
* **Miniature books**

Great Gifts for Kids

Any parent of young children will tell you, as if you didn't know, kids love Christmas. This holiday is looked forward to with even more anticipation than birthdays. "A dream," "enchanting," "magical"—these are the words my kids use to describe their favorite holiday. It is sometimes a challenge for parents to downplay the commercialism that surrounds Christmas and emphasize the true spirit of the season.

Kids love to be cozy during this wintry time of year, so I give mine bedding for Christmas: an **antique quilt, flannel sheets**, a **down comforter**. These are things they would eventually get anyway, but wrapping it up and putting it under the tree makes it more special.

Every year I give each of my children a Christmas ornament. Their favorites relate to their lives and interests: a school desk, a glass pickle, a canvas basketball shoe, a leather baseball mitt, an ice cream cone. By the time they leave home, they'll have the beginnings of a good collection. Some of my current favorites, including **24k gold mistletoe** ($11), a **maple leaf dipped in silver** ($9), and a set of twelve **glass raindrops** ($9), come from The Nature Company (800-227-1114, or visit one of their 100+ stores).

I make sure that at least one gift will provide the kids with something to do on Christmas Day after the presents are opened and the excitement has died down. Kits will occupy kids for hours; there are several fun ones at Hearthsong (800-325-2502), all for under $20, including **kits to make candles, clay jewelry, model airplanes, Christmas lollipops**, and a **bubble geometry set**.

Parents may appreciate a gift for their child that is educational or culturally enriching, as well as entertaining. The possibilities include **art supplies** of all kinds, **books, tickets to children's day at the symphony** or **to the ballet**—at least one visit to *The Nutcracker* is almost a requirement to graduate from childhood.

Every fall, a surfeit of new children's books is published in time for the holiday season. A lot of them are very good, but sometimes it's difficult to choose. It's hard to go wrong if you stick with the tried-and-true, the time-honored books you read and loved, or the ones that have come along since then to take their place among the classics. Particularly apt at Christmas time are ***The Polar Express*** by Chris Van Allsburg, ***A Child's***

Christmas in Wales by Dylan Thomas, *How the Grinch Stole Christmas* by Dr. Seuss, *A Christmas Carol* by Charles Dickens, and of course, *A Visit from Saint Nicholas* by Clement Moore. Non-Christmas-related books are always an appropriate gift; my personal favorites include:

*   *The Little Fur Family* and *Goodnight Moon* by Margaret Wise Brown
*   *Winnie-the-Pooh* and *The House at Pooh Corner* by A. A. Milne
*   *Curious George* by H. A. Rey
*   *The Tale of Peter Rabbit,* et al., by Beatrix Potter
*   *The Country Bunny and the Little Gold Shoes,* an Easter story by Dubose Hayward
*   *Madeline* by Ludwig Bemelmans
*   *Where the Wild Things Are* by Maurice Sendak
*   *Babar the King* by Jean de Brunhoff
*   *The Borrowers* by Mary Norton
*   *The Giving Tree* by Shel Silverstein
*   *Miss Rumphius* by Barbara Cooney
*   *The Secret Garden* by Frances Hodgson Burnett
*   *Alice's Adventures in Wonderland* by Lewis Carroll
*   *Stuart Little* and *Charlotte's Web* by E. B. White
*   *The Little House on the Prairie* by Laura Ingalls Wilder
*   *Tom Sawyer* and *Huckleberry Finn* by Mark Twain
*   *Anne of Green Gables* by Lucy Maud Montgomery
*   *The Wind in the Willows* by Kenneth Grahame
*   *The Hobbit* by J. R. R. Tolkien
*   *The Chronicles of Narnia* by C. S. Lewis
*   *Robinson Crusoe* by Daniel Defoe
*   *Treasure Island* by Robert Louis Stevenson
*   **Anything by Dr. Seuss**
*   *The Hardy Boys* by F. W. Dixon
*   *The Nancy Drew Mysteries* by Carolyn Keene

Many of these are available in the excellent catalog from Chinaberry Books, 800-776-2242.

You can create a great gift by combining a book with a related stuffed animal. One of the best I've seen recently is a **fluffy-furred rabbit** that can be turned completely inside out to reveal the older, wiser, smoother, more threadbare version in the book *The Velveteen Rabbit* ($27, Dandelion, 888-548-1968).

There's a fun and instructive new board game from England called **Bookworm** ($36), for ages six and up, that is designed to introduce your family to fine children's literature. (Whispering Pines, *Things for the Cabin* catalog, 800-836-4662).

You and your kids will love the whole series of **lateral thinking puzzle books** by Paul Sloane. You can buy these at local bookstores or find them in MindWare (800-999-0398), a catalog full of books and puzzles designed to stretch the brain and to entertain. Remember those little **plastic slide puzzles** you grew up with? They've got them here, only instead of numbers to rearrange, there are images of penguins and trout in 3-D (2 for $13.95). There are also **3-D jigsaw puzzles, dinosaur kits,** and the famous **cast-iron tavern puzzles** ($15.95). Everything in here is educational, but the emphasis is plainly on fun— these educational toys are not the types that'll make kids groan.

Children are natural-born scientists. Whether they're playing with soap bubbles or burning leaves with a magnifying glass, they are constantly experimenting and noting cause and effect. Your gift doesn't have to be glitzy to grab a child's interest. **A prism, magnetic marbles,** a **top**, a **gyroscope**, a **bug box**, a **dragon-fly eye**—many small gifts will encourage a sense of wonder. While you may think of a **Slinky** as a toy, it is actually physics in action. Give a child a refillable **candy kaleidescope** ($8, Dandelion, 888-548-1968) and watch her discover the world of prisms, mirrors, and reflection while happily munching. You might also want to consider a **microscope**, a **small telescope**, a **chemistry set**, a **crystal growing set**, or a pair of **binoculars**. All of these things will provide hours of fascination and exploration and most of them are reasonably priced at The Nature Company (800-227-1114) or in the catalog of American Science & Surplus (847-982-0870).

Children are also natural-born builders and inventors. Gifts in this category include basic **folding cardboard blocks, Legos and Duplos** (their oversized model for younger ones), **Erector sets, Lincoln Logs,** and **KNEX,** a building set made of rods and connectors.

In the Nick of Time

This holiday season you'll probably have all your shopping done before Halloween, just like you promised yourself last year when you were still wrapping packages at midnight on Christmas Eve, right? Just in case you break your vow and are left, once again, with last-minute gifts to buy, don't get stressed out.

One of the best places to look for last-minute gifts is your local bookstore. They've got calendars, journals, and literary gifts, in addition to the obvious: books for the sports enthusiast, children, the cook, the art lover, the business executive, the traveler—in other words, nearly everyone on your list.

Another quickie is to go to a newsstand that stocks an interesting assortment of magazines, choose one, and wrap it up after first filling out a subscription card.

Or head for the nearest drugstore, where you'll find possibilities for everyone, especially kids and teenagers: Walkman and Discman, blank tapes, toys and games, cosmetics and perfume, hair care products, photo frames, sporting goods, and stocking stuffers. You'll find all the components for a great gift basket that need not look as if it were thrown together in haste.

Gift certificates to many stores may be purchased through one site on the Web: 1-800-PRESENTS at www.1800presents.com.

If you're shopping by phone or on-line, here is a list of companies that offer overnight or second-day air delivery, for an additional charge—usually around $15:

Bloomingdale's by Mail, 800-777-0000 or
   www.bloomingdalesbymail.com
The Body Shop, 800-541-2535 or www.the-body-shop.com
Brookstone, 800-926-7000 or www.brookstoneonline.com
Crate and Barrel, 800-323-5461
The Disney Catalog, 800-237-5751 or www.disneystore.com
Eddie Bauer, 800-426-8020 or www.eddiebauer.com
Godiva, 800-846-3482 or www.godiva.com
Harry and David, 800-842-6111, or www.harryanddavid.com
J. Crew, 800-562-0258 or www.jcrew.com
L. L. Bean, 800-221-4221, or www.llbean.com
Orvis, 800-541-3541 or www.orvis.com
Patagonia, 800-638-6464 or www.patagonia.com
Pottery Barn, 800-922-5507
Sharper Image, 800-344-4444 or www.sharperimage.com
Signals, 800-669-9696
Tiffany's, 800-526-0649
Victoria's Secret, 800-888-8200
Williams-Sonoma, 800-541-2233 or www.williams-sonoma.com
Wireless, 800-669-9999 or www.giftcatalog.com

The people at Animal Town (800-445-8642) started their business to promote noncompetitive games. If you've ever been involved in a Monopoly game in which the players started throwing things and yelling at each other, you'll get their point right away. Many of their games, such as **A Treasure Hunt Through the Enchanted Forest**, stress cooperation; all players work toward the same goal.

There are dozens of other top-quality products in this catalog, including an **Art Supply Station** with watercolors, colored pencils, oil pastels, and brushes packed in a wooden suitcase ($40); the **perfect teddy bear** ($19); and a **kid-size croquet set** ($35). For the nature lover, they have the **Swiss Army compass** ($13); a **timber wolf puppet** ($36); and the **Pocket Survival Tool** ($14), a nifty little invention with "over 101 uses, including knife, screwdriver, bottle and can opener, saw, ruler, reamer, nut wrench, signal mirror, wire stripper, compass, and file."

If you're at a loss for gift ideas for the eight-and-under set, another good catalog to explore is Hand In Hand (800-872-9745). You'll find **musical instruments**, including a **child's guitar**, an **accordion**, and a **Chimalong**. And, along with art supplies, they sell several objects designed to be decorated by the child: **a light switch, lamp shade, peg rack**, and a **mug**.

For little ones who need a little encouragement to eat their oatmeal in the morning, the **Three Bears Porridge Bowl and Spoon Set** should make it a lot more fun. It includes an 8" handcrafted maple bowl and spoon, with a cinnamon/nutmeg grater, a stick of cinnamon, and a nutmeg kernel ($12.50, A Child's Dream, 800-359-2906).

A **red bicycle** is a classic kid's Christmas present. A **tricycle** or **scooter** is the right choice for a three-year-old, a 16" **bike with training wheels** will suit most five- or six-year-olds. Accessories are fun: an old-fashioned **handlebar bell** ($3.50–5 at Dandelion, 888-548-1968), a **tire pump**, or a **license plate** with the child's name on it. If you're giving a child her first bike and the grandparents ask for gift ideas, you could suggest a good **bike helmet**.

Remember Pluto Platters, those metal discs we used to sit on to ride down snowy hills? Now you can slide down the slopes in your **Snow-Shorts**, which have a foam-padded PVC seat built in and are designed to be worn over cold-weather gear. Available in two sizes for kids; the other for adults. ($29, Orvis, 800-541-3541)

Then there's always the beloved **Flexible Flyer Sled,** which hasn't been improved upon in over a hundred years. These sleds should come with a warning that dads are liable to steal them.

If toys are what you're after, you're better off sticking with the classics than trying to second-guess what's hot. Last year's Big Thing may be this year's Big Yawn. If you recall what you loved as a child, it's probably a good bet the children in your life will love it, too. And look at it this way: If they don't, you'll have a great time playing with it.

If you're interested in current kid picks, try calling the Duracell Holiday Toy Shopping hot line, 800-BEST TOYS, which will give you a recording of the ten most popular toys of the season, selected by the experts themselves: kids. Do be aware that this is a commercial plug for Duracell, so the list is skewed toward battery-operated toys. You'll find out what's in with the younger set, but you risk selecting something they already have or will get ten of from the other aunts and uncles.

How about a bright red, **miniature safe** with a real combination lock, just like the one you probably had, or wished you did, as a child? You'll find it in the Mind's Eye ($14.95, 800-949-3333), along with a lot of other nostalgic goodies, like the **brew-your-own root beer kit** ($12.95), a **red gum ball machine** ($24.95), and a **Magic 8-Ball** ($9.95) exactly like the one my brother gave me for Christmas when I was nine.

For a complete discussion of gifts especially for teenagers, see page 22.

Family Gifts

Much of the holiday gift exchange takes place between families. For those of us who have family members scattered across the country, it is often the only time of year we have any contact with our relatives, so it is difficult to know what to get for everyone, especially rapidly changing children. Rather than shop for each aunt, uncle, and cousin, it is sometimes easier, and more successful, to find a gift that will please the whole family. Food will do nicely: **fruit, fruit-of-the-month,** a **smoked turkey,** or an assortment of **cheeses and crackers.** The Williams-Sonoma holiday catalog (800-541-2233) is a thick, annual edition filled with festive foods and gift baskets, so if you need help, start here.

When I was growing up, a family friend gave us a **board game** every year on Christmas Eve, and it became our tradition to spend the evening playing our new game while listening to radio reports of Santa's progress from the North Pole. You can encourage family togetherness with games the whole family can play. Younger kids will enjoy **checkers, Candyland, Chutes and Ladders,** and **Monopoly Junior.** The original **Monopoly, Balderdash, Clue, Scattergories, Yahtzee,** and **Scrabble** are favorites for ages eight and up. A **jigsaw puzzle** or **poker chips, a deck of cards,** and a copy of *Hoyle's Rules of Games* are other game gifts which can involve the whole family. Consider the **7-in-1 Wooden Game Set,** which includes checkers, chess, backgammon, draughts, and dominoes, plus a set of playing cards and poker dice, with a book of rules and instructions ($49, Norm Thompson, 800-547-1160).

Or choose a book the whole family will enjoy. This could be an **almanac,** *The Guinness Book of World Records, The Secret Language of Birthdays* by Gary Goldschneider ($34.95, Penguin Studio), or **a coffee-table book** about a favorite family vacation destination. A few other gifts for the whole family:

* **A picnic basket,** filled with a picnic cloth, napkins, and fun food
* **The family genealogy**
* **A calendar**
* **A Christmas tree, a wreath, or holiday centerpiece of greens** delivered to the door (Smith & Hawken, 800-776-3336; be sure to arrange for early-December delivery)
* **A popcorn popper and a supply of popcorn,** still on the cob (look at your local farmer's market)
* **An old-fashioned hand-crank ice cream maker** ($155, Sur La Table, 800-243-0852) and an assortment of toppings
* **A donation made in their name to a charitable cause** (see page 114)
* **Outdoor games** (badminton, smashball, croquet, volleyball)
* **Tickets to the theater, ballet, or a sporting event**
* **A photo album**

* **A shiitake mushroom log** ($30, Seeds of Change, 888-762-7333). These items are truly amazing—all you do, literally, is add water, and practically overnight you have a crop of delicious mushrooms.
* **A birdhouse**, a **bird feeder**, a **bag of seed**, and a **field guide** to help with identification
* **A Sonic-Care electric toothbrush**
* **A credit card–sized Olympus camera and a lot of film**

Gifts for Grown-ups

While children experience the magic of Christmas, many adults perceive it as an obligation that often threatens to eclipse the true spirit of the season. When considering gifts for the grown-ups on your shopping list, think of things that will soothe frazzled nerves and help restore feelings of "goodwill to all."

Warm as Toast

The holiday season signifies short days, cold nights, and an inclination to hibernate. Snuggly gifts, from a **hot water bottle** to a **cashmere bathrobe**, will hit the spot. **Wool mufflers** are yummy, great for him or her, and they won't break the bank.

Encourage a long, relaxing soak in a hot bath with a gift of the Cozy Weather Blend of **Tub Tea**. Lavender, calendula, cinnamon, and cloves combine to warm the body and soothe the senses. Just drop an oversized tea bag into the bath as it fills. Three bags are $12, or you can choose a gift box that includes all five blends: Everyday, Full Moon, Hot Afternoon, Cozy Weather, and Romance ($20, Restoration Hardware). Wrap up the Tub Tea with a copy of *The Art of the Bath* by Sara Slavin and Carl Petzke ($18.95, Chronicle Books).

Candles of all kinds make great gifts that can be pressed into service right away to enhance the holiday atmosphere. Put together a collection of chunky natural beeswax candles from Pottery Barn (call 800-922-5507 to order, or to find the store nearest you) or colorful tapers from Illuminations (800-226-3537).

Fill a basket with new-crop **walnuts in the shell**, accompanied by a **bottle of port** and some **Stilton cheese**, with a note encouraging the gift recipient to sit in front of the fireplace and take time to crack, sip, and munch. Williams-Sonoma (800-541-2233) can supply a whole Stilton ($49.50) and a handsome stainless steel **English Ratchet Nutcracker** ($24).

Cordwood, kindling, a **log rack** ($115, J. Peterman, 800-231-7341), a **kindling ax, long matches** for lighting the fire, or **fireplace tools** will be warmly received. Restoration Hardware has a canvas **log carrier** ($19), a **gas match** ($29), and heavy-duty, red suede **fireplace gloves** ($13.50). A thick pile cotton **fireside blanket** from Harmony ($75, 800-456-1177) is another cozy gift anyone would love.

For the ultimate in toasty toes, give everyone on your list the **Foot Duvet**, one-size-fits-all duck-down booties with cotton lining ($20), from Restoration Hardware (call 800-762-1005 for the store nearest you). Or, **After Dinner Socks** to sit by the fire in. Made of heavy, mohair angora, they're available in yummy colors: peach, pale yellow, light blue, lime green, red, and purple ($32 at Summer House, a must-see store in Mill Valley, CA, 415-383-6695).

More cozy gifts include the following:

* **Shearling mittens**
* **Polarfleece gloves**
* **A bright red union suit**
* **A velvet scarf**
* **Mink or faux fur ear muffs**
* **An electrically heated towel rack**
* **A down comforter**
* **A French wool beret** (available in ten terrific colors, $20 at Niebaum-Coppola Estate Winery, 707-968-1135)
* **Sheepskin slippers**
* **Polarfleece throw**

Small but Special Gifts

Sometimes we want to give just a little special something that bespeaks the holidays. Perhaps you've been invited to an open house, or you want to remember your neighbors, the parents of your children's friends, your child's teacher, or other people you see often during the year. Among my favorite small gifts are delicacies from the kitchen: grandmother's recipe for **Bourbon balls, tangerine marmalade, lemon curd, olive oil infused with herbs, spiced pecans, homemade wine,** a **steamed persimmon pudding, imported olives in a Provençal crock, herbal tea tucked into a tea pot,** and, of course, the ever-popular plate of **holiday cookies and candies.**

For an unusual—but very traditional—gift, stitch a tiny pouch of gold mesh fabric and fill it with **frankincense** and **myrrh** to make a beautiful allusion to the gifts of the Three Wise Men. The contents can be burned as incense to give the house a delightful holiday fragrance. (Frankincense and myrrh are available in the bulk herb section of large natural foods retailers such as Whole Foods.)

Mulling spices make a wonderful holiday hostess gift, and a great gift for yourself if you're entertaining during this season. You can brew stove-top in a pot of simmering cider or red wine to make the whole house smell like Christmas. You'll find these at kitchen stores such as Williams-Sonoma, and probably at your local grocery store.

You can make a beautiful and inexpensive gift presentation by planting a **hyacinth bulb** in a 3-inch clay pot with a saucer beneath. Top the soil with Spanish moss, tie the pot with a French wire ribbon bow, and place it in a cellophane bag with excelsior in the bottom. Tie the bag with twine and attach a tag with care instructions.

Deck the Halls

Christmas trees, garlands, mistletoe, wreaths, boughs and centerpieces of greenery, dried flowers and fruit, and **ribbon** will help make anyone's home festive. If you're giving one of these as a gift to someone out of town, be sure to have it shipped early and opened upon receipt. The Williams-Sonoma (800-541-2233) **bay leaf wreath** is tried-and-true; it looks and smells wonderful when it arrives, and it improves with age as the leaves dry and curl. At only $23.50, you can afford to send it to everyone on your list. Now, they've added a **wreath made of freshly harvested olive branches** ($29), which is destined to join the bay leaf wreath as a classic. Smith & Hawken (800-776-3336) always has an outstanding selection of more elaborate holiday wreaths.

I love giving **paperwhite narcissus, amaryllis,** and **hyacinth**

Gifts That Make a Difference

* **Until They Find a Cure Bracelet** from The Body Shop ($20, most of the proceeds go to AIDS research).
* **Gift of Life Greeting Cards,** twenty-five for a donation of $125 (Susan G. Komen Breast Cancer Foundation, 214-450-1784).
* **Alternative Gifts International**, 800-842-2243. This catalog is full of wonder-working gifts for people around the world: $50 will plant half an acre of soybeans to help feed the hungry people of Bangladesh; $18 will buy cancer medicine for young victims of the Chernobyl disaster in the Ukraine; $60 will buy one reconditioned wheelchair for a Bosnian child, crippled by a land mine or bullet.
* **Seva Foundation**. Their gifts of service, starting at $30, help people around the world who are struggling to meet basic needs (800-223-7382).
* **Membership to a local public radio station.**
* **Resource Renewal Institute**, advocates of Green Plan, a solution to our environmental degradation, 415-928-3774.
* **Habitat for Humanity**, 800-334-3308. Jimmy Carter's project to build homes for needy families.
* **Humane Society gift certificate** for a kitten or puppy. If it turns out you guessed wrong, and the person chooses not to adopt, you've contributed to a good cause anyway.
* **Barnes & Noble Children's Holiday Book Drive**. Donate a new book at one of their stores; they'll match it, and distribute the books to disadvantaged children.
* **International Wildlife Coalition**, 508-548-8328. The Whale Adoption Project allows you to choose a specific whale they've been tracking. They'll send a photo, description, and information to the child you designate for $17.

bulbs for indoor forcing. Your gift recipient will have the fun of planting the bulbs, then watching them grow, and finally the satisfaction of seeing cheerful blooms in the dead of winter. Be sure to accompany the gift with an appropriate container and instructions. These are virtually foolproof—even the proverbial black thumb will have success.

Gifts for Seniors

Seniors often feel loneliest at this time of year, when families gather. If they are able to travel, arrange for a brief visit—long enough to renew ties, but not to wear them out with the exuberance of younger people. If they can no longer get about easily, take a few days of your holiday to go to them with a little good cheer.

Many gifts in the Warm As Toast section (page 111) of this chapter will be appropriate for the seniors in your life. If they are sedentary, they may suffer from poor circulation and chronic chilliness, so anything cozy and warming will be appreciated.

Older people with arthritis in their hands will enjoy a collection of **kitchen tools** with large, comfort-grip, nonslip handles. This set includes a grater, peeler, jar opener, kitchen shears, ice cream scoop, can opener, and hanging rack ($50, Brookstone, 800-351-7222).

How long has it been since they had their picture taken? Give mom and/or dad a **session with a photographer**. Better yet, plan a photo including all the generations. You can take care of framing the photos and help distribute them to other siblings.

Many older people have health problems or are on restricted diets. You can promote an interest in health by giving them a **cookbook** or **gift basket** of foods that meets their dietary needs**, membership to a health club**, a **juicer**, or a **blood pressure monitor**. Encourage them to get out and walk with a gift of a **fanny pack** (there's a good one at Title Nine Sports, 510-655-5999, that holds all the usual, plus a 20-ounce water bottle, $26) and a **pedometer**, to measure how far they've gone (available at most sporting goods stores for around $15).

Gifts That Keep on Giving

Subscriptions are great gifts because the recipient gets a holiday present, then a package every month, and you will be remembered fondly at least that often. If your gift is a hit, you can renew it for next year. Choose an unusual **magazine** or special **newspaper subscription**, or a Something-of-the-Month. Many of these are set up to begin in December and some have three-month and six-month options. The company that probably started the whole thing is Harry and David (800-547-3033), and their **Fruit of the Month Club** is still terrific. Some other favorites include:

✻ **The Personal Book Club**. You can send biographies and histories to your father, or spy novels to your son; a grandmother may request the best in children's literature for her grandchildren each month. Describe the gift recipient in detail, and this fine bookseller will make choices accordingly, gift-wrap the books, and send them every month or bi-monthly. You may want to sign up at the same time; this sounds like heaven! To get started, write, fax, or e-mail The Book Passage (51 Tamal Vista Boulevard, Corte Madera, CA 94925, fax: 415-924-3838, or e-mail: messages2bookpassage.com.), winner of the American Booksellers Association Bookseller of the Year Award for 1996.

✻ **Boxer of the Month Club** from Celebration Fantastic (800-235-3272). One hundred percent cotton boxer shorts are decorated with seasonal images: jack-o'-lanterns for October, turkey and pumpkin pie for November, and of course, hearts for February. This gift is available for three months, six months, or twelve months, and if you order for the whole year, you'll get a bonus of birthday boxers at just the right time.

✻ **Three Months of Fine Cheeses**. In three different shipments, approximately six weeks apart, your gift recipient will receive a wooden crate filled with three different superb offerings from artisan cheesemakers in England and America. M-m-m-m! ($152, Williams-Sonoma, 800-541-2233)

✻ **A Year of Candlelight**. Your lucky recipient will receive frosted, lidded canister candles in seasonal colors and fragrances to match each month, including Refreshing Rain in April, Rootbeer Float in August, and Pumpkin Pie in November (Illuminations, 800-CANDLES).

* **Bath of the Month Club** (800-406-BATH, or www.mudbath.com.spa). A start-up kit ($29.95 plus shipping and handling) includes Fango Mud Bath powder imported from the spa at Abano Terme, Italy; one pound of Sarvar Sea Salts with French organic peppermint imported from Hungary; and a 4-ounce bottle of Eucalyptus Oil Bath therapy. Then, for an additional $9 per month, your giftee receives two to four spa products: Rain and Bath Shower Gel, Tension Relief Foot and Body Soak, and Mustard Rub. What a great idea!

* **Starbucks Seasonal Celebration Tour** ($80, Starbucks, 800-STARBUC). They'll send four shipments of two 1-pound bags of their delicious coffee beans and blends, geared to harmonize with the four seasons.

* **Three months of crated bulbs**, including December Paperwhites, January Red Tulips, and February Narcissus ($99, Smith & Hawken, 800-776-3336).

* **Twelve months of potted tropical plants**, including Passion Flower and Bird of Paradise; just tell them what month you want to start. ($195, Langenbach, 800-362-1991).

* **Mrs. Field's Cookie of the Month Club** (800-344-CHIP). Mrs. Field's will send a tin of one dozen cookies of your choice for three months, six months, or twelve months.

* **Cake of the Month Club**, including Chocolate Velvet Truffle Cake, Lemon Poppy Seed Cake, and Banana Chocolate Chip Cake sent to you by Miss Grace Lemon Cake Co., 800-FOR-CAKE.

* **Bagel of the Month**. Get monthly delivery of two dozen ($39) to twelve dozen ($139) of New York's finest from H & H Bagels, 800-NY-BAGEL.

* **Wines of the Month Club**. Available through my favorite wine purveyor, the Mill Valley Market Wine Shop (800-699-4634), members receive two bottles per month, usually a red and a white, along with tasting notes and a short bio for each wine. Selections are from all over, not just California and France, and they will tailor to suit your tastes. Two levels of membership are offered: $20 a month and $30 a month, and wines are offered at the case bottle price.

* **The Monthly Cigar Club** (800-89-TASTE). This club offers a selection of four premium cigars from manufacturers in the leading cigar-producing countries including Honduras, Nicaragua, and the

Dominican Republic; brands like Partagas, Don Jivan, Cohiba, and Tabacon. *The Stogie Newsletter* accompanies each monthly shipment, as well as offers for exclusive discounts on future cigar orders.

* **Fly of the Month Club.** This one's for the angling fanatic in your life. Each month he'll receive three hand-tied, ready-to-fish, freshwater flies like the ancient Red Hackle, which dates back to A.D. 300, the stunning Gray Ghost, or the legendary Blue Quill. A written history of each classic pattern is beautifully presented with an onionskin overlay (six months $69.95, full year, $129.95); contact the *Fishing Enthusiast* for more details (800-597-0634) or look at their website at 222.planet-fish.pair.com).

* **Twelve Months of Micro-Brewery Beer.** Each month, your giftee will receive two six-packs of micro-brewery beer from two different small brewers, chosen from among the tops in the country, along with recipes and information about the breweries and the beer ($15.95 per month, Hogshead Beer Sellers, 800-795-BEER, or order on-line at www.hogshead.com).

* **Pasta of the Month Club.** For $20 a month Flying Noodle will send two gourmet pastas, two sauces, and recipes (800-566-0599).

* **Potato of the Month.** These are not your average spuds. New Penny Farm (800-827-7551) will ship you such exotics as Bintje, Shepody, and Green Mountain, 5 pounds of a different variety every month, packed in a burlap bag.

* **Muffin of the Month Club** (800-742-2403). Have six seasonally inspired muffins delivered monthly via FedEx the day they are baked. Look for Chocolate Cream Cheese in February, Pumpkin in October, and Rum Raisin in December.

* **The Tea Club.** Send shipments ($11.95 per month) of two different selections of tea, including the rare black tea, Chinese Panyang Congou; "Garden of Sparrows," the fanciest Formosa Oolong; and a range of green, white, and herbal teas ($11.95 a month, 800-FULL-LEAF).

* **Spice of the Month Club** (888-8-SPICES) features exotic herbs and spices, such as Madagascar vanilla beans, yellow poppy seeds, Sri Lankan cinnamon quills, golden-tipped marjoram. Each month your gift recipient will receive two selections, suggestions for use, and a description of the next month's choices.

* **The Crossword Club** (800-874-8100). You can send six cross-

word puzzles per month, of the same caliber as the Sunday *New York Times* puzzle, plus the solution to the previous puzzle ($35, also available in large type for $55).

Remembering the Less Fortunate

Some good people make giving to the needy a focus of their holiday season. One woman sent a letter to all of her friends and said, "This year, rather than sending me a present, I'd like for you to take the time you would have spent shopping for me and do something to treat yourself (go to a concert, take a bubblebath). Then take the money you would have spent on my gift, and use it for someone who needs it. I'd love to hear what you did." The response was overwhelming. One friend bought several pairs of winter gloves and gave them out to needy people she saw on her Christmas rounds. Another couple bought a bag of groceries and donated it to their local food bank. A teacher helped one of his students buy a ticket so she could go home for the holidays, rather than spend Christmas in the dorm alone. This is truly a gift that keeps on giving.

Instead of exchanging family gifts, you can decide as a group to provide Christmas for another family who would otherwise do without. You may find needy families by contacting a nearby day-care center, your place of worship, the social services office in your community, a battered women's shelter, or a shelter for the homeless. Try to find out the children's ages and include goodies, as well as more practical things, like warm clothing and books. Ask for a wish list.

Another friend buys two of everything when doing her holiday grocery shopping and gives away the duplicate fixings to someone in need: an AIDS patient, a single mom, a homeless shelter.

7

Rites of Passage

and Personal Achievements

Every now and then, I hear someone lament that there are no rites of passage today as there were in ancient times and cultures. I disagree. There are many occasions in our lives based on social and religious traditions—and biological realities, for that matter—that constitute rites of passage in the truest sense of the term. And if you still find that rites of passage are lacking in your life or the lives of those close to you, it is possible to create your own.

Graduation Gifts

School graduation ceremonies are an important milestone for children. Many families today stress the importance of education, and graduation is an excellent time to acknowledge a young person for a job well done.

Preschool, Kindergarten, and Grade School Graduation

Graduation is now celebrated at all different levels of educational achievement, not just to mark the completion of high school and college, as it once was. In our culture, we expect our children to graduate from preschool and kindergarten, and it is not necessary to make too big a thing of it, but it is nice to note it. The gift doesn't have to be elaborate or expensive. In fact, some of the most thoughtful gifts don't have to cost a thing.

Preschool, kindergarten, and elementary school graduation can best be celebrated by being there, taking photos, and letting the child know how proud you are. A small gift, ideally one that pertains to school, is optional but appropriate. You could give a new **backpack,** a **book,** a set of **art supplies,** or a **card** with a personal note.

Middle School Graduation

For many children, graduation from middle school is an important step toward adulthood. As a result, there is a little more emphasis placed on graduation at the middle school level than there is at the grade school level. Children, especially girls, dress up for the occasion, which means a new **dress and accessories.** There is usually a dance following the commencement ceremonies, which means yet another new dress. Grandparents might offer to buy one of the outfits, or pay to **have her hair done,** as their gift. Taking the new graduate out for **lunch or dinner** is a fitting way to celebrate the occasion. In advance of graduation, you can supply a small **journal** for friends and teachers to sign or reminisce in. Gifts can be skewed to summer activities: a new **fishing pole,** a **special camp,** a **camera.** They might also reflect the tastes of a new, more grown-up person: **books,** a **computer,** or **desk accessories** in preparation for high school.

High School Graduation

High school graduation, while we still expect it of our kids, is considered more of a milestone. It marks the beginning of taking on the greater responsibilities of adulthood, either as a student or as a working person. It may also signify leaving home for the first time.

High school graduation is also a significant event in the lives of parents. Suddenly seventeen or eighteen years seems like such a very short time and many parents approach high school graduation with a mixture of pride and loss.

One single dad gave his son a **graduation party** at home and set up a sort of shrine to his childhood. It consisted of a glass case filled with mementos, including his first shoes, his baseball mitt, class photos through the years, pictures of the senior prom, and photographs of him with his mother and father throughout the years. I cried when I saw it and I barely knew the boy, so I know he must have been moved by his father's tribute.

You may want to mitigate these feelings of loss, and bring a little levity to the situation with a gift like *Where's Mom Now That I Need Her?* by Betty, Kathryn, and Kent Frandsen ($12.95, Aspen West Publishing), the definitive guide to living away from home. It is basically a cookbook of fast, easy, nutritious recipes, plus a stain removal guide, a first aid section, and hints on grocery shopping, clothing repair, and everything else moms do so well.

If someone else's recipes just won't cut it, put together **your own cookbook** for your fledglings and give them each a copy as they leave the nest. This is a gift to be compiled over the years, a little bit at a time. It will include their favorite recipes, such as Saturday morning buttermilk pancakes and Snickerdoodles, as well as foolproof how-to-impress-a-date recipes like Lemon Chicken with Roasted Potatoes. Speaking strategically, you will leave out a few important ones like your Black Bean Chile recipe that they have come to count on week after week. This way they'll have a reason to call or come home.

From the people who brought you the Baby Time Capsule, there's now the **Graduation Time Capsule**. This gift might be a little "young" for college grads but just right for high school seniors, particularly girls, who tend to be a bit more sentimental. It includes Messages to the Future, a book called *What Life Was Like My Senior Year*, and a "capsule" in which to collect memorabilia. The whole thing is then sealed, to be opened on a designated date in the future, perhaps a ten-year reunion. ($19.95, The Original Time Capsule Company, 800-729-8463)

The **Hand-Tied Bouquet** from 1-800-FLOWERS is a beautiful gift to give a girl graduate as she steps from the podium after receiving her diploma. It will stay fresh for a week, and then air-dry beautifully to become a keepsake of the occasion. (When it's all over, she can put it in her time capsule.)

Parents or grandparents of new grads: If you've ever had a mind to give your child or grandchild a new **car**, there will probably never be a better time.

As a gift to your graduate who is leaving home for the first time, you can wrap up **your favorite article of clothing** that they always borrow. They'll probably take it anyway, so you might as well make a gift of it, so it can serve as a warm reminder of you whenever they wear it.

If you're a saver, and you possess modest sewing skills, you can stitch up a **quilt** using the grad's old T-shirts. Cotton jersey sheets are all the rage, and this quilt would be even cozier.

A **subscription to the hometown newspaper** will help them stay in touch with the news from back home while they learn to feel at home in a new place.

A **computer** will probably be at the top of the college-bound high school graduate's wish list, if he or she doesn't already have one. Equally important in my book: a good **dictionary, thesaurus**, and **world atlas**. Another indispensable tome: *The New York Public Library Desk Reference* ($40, Macmillan General Reference), which includes easy to access information on everything, including the kitchen sink.

Another book they'll never know how they lived without: *Life's Big Instruction Book* by Carol Orsay Madigan ($29.95, Warner Books). It provides practical information for everyday survival—everything from a guide to basic pasta shapes, to opera for beginners. Almost as good as having a parent around.

You can target your grad gift to their new digs, which will need outfitting with the basics whether it be a dorm room or first apartment. Fill a **laundry hamper**, a **wastebasket**, or **stackable storage crates** with such necessities as a **CD holder**, a **telephone**, and a **desk lamp**. Hold Everything (800-421-2264) is a good source for most of these items.

The first time they need to hang a picture, or install the stereo, they'll appreciate your gift of a tool kit, complete with **hammer, socket wrenches, screwdriver, nails, hooks, tape measure, flashlight**, and **duct tape**.

No doubt, they already own a hair dryer, but other small appliances they can begin to collect include a **toaster** or **toaster oven**, a **coffee maker**, a **popcorn popper**, a **Dust Buster**, and an **iron**. You can shop for most of these things at the local hardware or department store.

Another idea for the soon-to-be dorm resident: a thick, mono-grammed **terry robe**. There are many on the market, but none better than the Egyptian cotton one at Hammacher Schlemmer ($99.95, 800-543-3366). A monogrammed **bath sheet** is sure to come in handy, no matter where the graduate is headed ($26, The Company Store, 800-285-3696).

And don't forget the always useful **bath bucket**. Many dorms fea-ture communal bathrooms that may be down the hall from the stu-dent's room. Fill a galvanized aluminum or plastic bucket (customize it by adding drainage holes to the bottom) with **hair care products**, a **natural sea sponge**, a **bath mitt, soap, razor**, and **shaving cream**, and your gift will see daily use.

Prepaid telephone calling cards or **gasoline credit cards** are grad gifts that will be received with gratitude.

On a less practical side—and a lot of fun to give and receive—are college kid "toys," such as a **backgammon set**, a **dart board**, a **deck of cards**, a **gum ball machine**, or a **jump rope**. These are great ice breakers with the new dorm mates.

College Graduation

College graduation or completion of graduate school is an even big-ger accomplishment, and so deserves a gift of greater import. If the graduate will be assuming an office job, she'll appreciate a **leather brief case**, perhaps with a copy of the *Wall Street Journal* (800-568-7625) tucked in, and **a year's subscription**. Other useful subscriptions might be *Fortune* (800-621-8000), *Money* (800-633-9970), *Business Week* (800-635-1200), *Time* (800-541-1000), and *Newsweek* (800-631-1040). Personalized or monogrammed **memo pads** can be purchased from your local printing shop. **Desk accessories** or a leather **mouse pad** ($25, Colorado Pen Company, 800-766-PENS) can be used at work or in the home office.

For the graduate who is as yet unemployed, you may be able to help in the process of job-hunting by giving a **gift certificate for a profes-**

sional résumé-writing service. A set of clothes to wear to interviews will hopefully pay dividends, too.

If time (theirs) and budget (yours) allow, you may want to finance a trip—New York, Belize, London, the Grand Canyon—for a few days or a few months. Tuck the ticket into a guidebook (see page 54). Many kids set off on the Grand Tour, so a **Eurorail Pass** (800-722-7151) makes a terrific gift, but if it isn't in your budget, try **hiking boots**, a sturdy **backpack**, a **travel journal**, or a trusty **Swiss Army knife**. There are numerous trips that offer opportunities for learning: archeological digs, photographic safaris. The Museum of Natural History sponsors several such trips through their adventure travel department (800-462-8687). A trip with a wilderness travel group (there are several throughout the country) would be a great way to clear the head after four years of academic pursuits.

Start a **stock portfolio** or an **Individual Retirement Account** in their name; they'll be grateful later. Or, a gift of ready **cash** may be just what they need now to get on their feet.

If you're looking for a humorous gift, you can give your graduate an embroidered **pillow** featuring his school colors and the slogan, "It's hard to be humble when you're from the University of V/S " ($34), or **boxer shorts** with a cap and gown design and, "I did it!" written on them ($16, both from Celebration Fantastic, 800-235-3272). **Monopoly** now makes games specifically geared to particular universities. If your grad is sentimental about her alma mater, call the campus bookstore to see if it stocks this game.

Graduate School Completion

Finishing an advanced degree is an accomplishment few people ever achieve, and those who do deserve a lot of credit for their perseverence and hard work. All of the gift ideas for college graduates apply as well to those who have completed graduate school. The post-grad has probably earned a well-deserved **vacation** after all those years of hard work, so all of the travel suggestions listed above may be of particular relevance.

If someone you know has finally finished law school you'll find the perfect gift in For Counsel (800-637-0098). This catalog offers everything from serious **lawyer ties**, to **barrister boxer shorts**, to irreverent

lawyer tee-shirts. They also have **videos** of all the great lawyer films, including *To Kill a Mockingbird, Twelve Angry Men*, and *Anatomy of a Murder*. There are also several products specifically for the female lawyer, including **scarves** and **jewelry**.

A recent C.P.A. will probably enjoy a copy of the **1040 tax form rendered in solid chocolate**, or a **Powerful IRS Protection Candle**, which comes with a detailed ritual. Both are available from For Counsel.

Medical school is grueling so a little comic relief and a lot of congratulations are in order upon completion. You'll find plenty of the former in *The New Yorker Book of Doctor Cartoons* ($10, Knopf).

Coming of Age

Our culture has very little in the way of ritual surrounding the Coming of Age, the time when hormonal changes take place in boys and girls that signify their entrance into adulthood. Outside of certain religious ceremonies, such as bar and bat mitzvahs (see page 133), most Americans lack a tradition for celebrating the passage from childhood to adulthood, so take it upon yourself to start your own.

In our family, we have a coming-of-age tradition that takes place around the fourteenth birthday: Our children **spend two weeks climbing in the Sierras** with Outward Bound (800-243-8520), a wilderness school for teens and adults. The experience is intense. In addition to being physically grueling, it demands a lot emotionally: participants spend twenty-four hours on a "solo," alone with just their journals. They return subtly changed by this powerful experience, which gives participants a lasting sense of independence and competence.

If you've kept a **Birthday Yearbook** (see page 10) a coming-of-age ceremony is an ideal time to present it to your son or daughter (you can still add to it later). If you haven't kept up a book through the years, now is the time to put together a **scrapbook/journal** of memories of the past, advice for the future from you and other elders, and photographs of childhood.

Sweet Sixteen and
First Driver's License

In most states, the sixteenth birthday is an important coming of age, the age when most teens can legally obtain their driver's licenses. A gift of a **key chain** can be both useful and symbolic of their expanding independence. My favorite is the classic **sterling silver screwball key ring** from Tiffany's ($40, plus engraving, 800-526-0649), which you can have engraved with initials on one side, and the all-important birth date on the other. Be sure to allow three to four weeks for the engraving. If the person in question will be driving one of your cars, you can copy the key and put it on the key ring before you wrap it.

Give him or her a **tee-shirt** with the fitting slogan: "I'm 16! Give me the keys. Give me the credit cards and get out of my way." (The Lighter Side, 941-747-2356).

Practically speaking, if she's getting her own car, give her an **emergency kit** for the trunk, with flares, jumper cables, a flashlight, and a gas can. You can assemble the components of this gift at an auto supply store, or get the **Roadside Safety Kit** from Restoration Hardware ($25, 800-762-1005).

It may sound crazy, but one veteran parent sends his kids to **race car driving school**, insisting that if they learn to handle a car at high speed, they can handle it anywhere. He swears the classes have saved their lives. They are not cheap, nor are they available everywhere, but if you have a NASCAR racetrack in your area, you can call for information. I know several sixteen-year-old boys who would be thrilled with this gift.

Sweet Sixteen is a sentimental birthday, and it's a perfect time to pass down a **family heirloom**. This is an occasion for significant jewelry; she is no longer a little girl, and **pearl** or **diamond earrings** can begin her collection of adult jewels. **Birthstone jewelry** is especially appropriate for Sweet Sixteen (see page 33 for a list). Fortunoff's, the New York institution (800-FORTUNOFF), is the place to look if you're fresh out of heirlooms and want to shop for one.

One young friend thought her dad was the best when he rented a **limousine** for her sixteenth birthday, so that he could take her and three friends out for a night in San Francisco: dinner and the theater.

Needless to say, he had a very good time, too. It takes a pretty cool dad to pull this off.

New American Citizen

If you know someone who has just become an American citizen, you can help him or her celebrate by giving an **American flag**, or a copy of the **Constitution** and the **Bill of Rights**, available through the National Archives in Washington, D.C. (800-234-8861). An **atlas** of their newly adopted country is also a fitting gift, as is a **book about U.S. history**.

Retirement

Retirement after many years of service to the same company is classically celebrated with the gift of a **gold watch**. This is a terrific gift, and entirely appropriate, but today's retirement gifts might be better skewed toward the future. People are retiring younger and healthier, and rather than marking the end of a long career as it once did, retirement now celebrates the beginning of a new phase of life, likely underscored by good health and more freedom to pursue hobbies and travel. Gifts to support this new point of view might include a subscription to *Travel & Leisure* (800-888-8728) or a **guidebook** to an exotic destination. Even better, **send them somewhere they've always wanted to go**, like a cruise to the Greek Islands.

Today's retirees have more time to enjoy the outdoors and observe the elements, and might appreciate an **indoor-outdoor thermometer**, a **rain gauge**, a **sundial**, **wind chimes**, a **barometer**, or a full-fledged **weather station**. There are several to choose from in the catalog of Wind and Weather, 800-922-9463. Check with The Nature Company, 800-227-1114, for a wide range of **telescopes** and **star-gazing guides**.

Bird watching might be fun, now that they have more time on their hands. Equip them with **binoculars**, a **Peterson's Field Guide**, and a good **walking stick**. Or they could have fun from their living room window with a backyard **birdhouse**, or a **bird feeder** that adheres to the window with suction cups.

Hook up your retired friends or relatives with **Elderhostel** (617-

426-8056), a nonprofit institution dedicated to serving the educational needs of Americans over fifty-five years of age. You can offer to pay the tuition for one of their **classes**, which typically lasts between one and four weeks, with accommodations available on or near the campus of more than 2,000 participating institutions throughout the United States, Canada, and seventy foreign countries. If you would like to pique someone's interest, call Elderhostel to order a free catalog or a video ($6). Most programs are about $340 for one week, which beats the cost of camp.

If the person is physically fit and adventurous, a great group gift might be a new **mountain bike** and the accoutrements: **a helmet, gloves**, a **biking shirt, water bottle**, and **Power Bars**.

Retirement may be anticipated as a time to take it easy and loaf a little, in which case a **hammock** and a good **book** might be just the thing. Audio Editions (see page 140) is a great source for **books on tape**. Leisure time also affords the opportunity for more elaborate culinary pursuits; you can facilitate this with the gift of a **cookbook** or **cooking classes**.

Recent retirees may welcome more time for personal reflection. There is a wonderful book, *Legacy: A Step-by-Step Guide to Writing a Personal History* by Linda Spence ($14.95, Swallow Press), which will encourage and help them write their memoirs. When they've finished, they can give copies to family members—personally, I can't imagine a more thoughtful gift.

And, in case the retiree is short on ideas about what to do with all his spare time and has a good sense of humor, give him a volume called *2001 Things to Do Before You Die* by Dane Sherwood ($6.95, Harper-Collins), a checklist of wonderful, ridiculous, crazy, and inspiring things to achieve before our time in this world is up.

(For more discussion of retirement gifts, see page 164.)

Religious Occasions

In certain religious traditions, rites of passage rituals—including baptism, confirmation, and bar mitzvah—have been honored for centuries. When your friends and acquaintances celebrate these occasions, you may want to participate, but often it is difficult for a person outside the religion to know what gift is appropriate.

Gifts for the Golfer

* Tiffany's larger-than-life **Golf Ball paperweight** in full lead crystal ($50, 800-526-0649).
* *On the Green*, a leather-bound golf tally book ($20, Kate's Paperie 800-809-9880).
* **Chocolate Golf Balls** (set of three, $13, Godiva, 800-9-GODIVA).
* Pro Sham, a **chamois golf towel** with brass grommet to attach to bag ($19.95, Herrington, 800-903-2878).
* For the traveling golfer: a **zippered black leather case** with a screw-together putter, two golf balls, and a wooden cup—presto—hotel golf ($50, Dandelion, 888-548-1968).
* **Golf club key ring** in sterling silver ($55, Tiffany's, 800-526-0649).
* A plush **Tiger Golf Club Headcover** ($24.98, The Lighter Side, 941-747-2356).
* **Potty Putting**—plastic "grass" mat to place in front of the toilet, contoured like a real green, complete with a hole, plastic putter, and two plastic balls ($17.98, The Lighter Side, 941-747-2356).
* **Tiddly Golf**. Yes, a tabletop combination of tiddly winks and golf ($21, Dandelion, (888-548-1968).
* **A great golf book**. (The Classics of Golf, 800-339-0745, has numerous titles to choose from.)
* *Shakespeare on Golf* by John Tullius and Joe Ortiz ($21.95, Hyperion), a hilarious compendium of golfing wit and wisdom from the Bard himself.
* A set of **six St. Andrews golf balls** imprinted with the crest from the venerable Scottish home of the game ($19.50, Eximious, 800-221-9464).

* A **Golf Ball Champagne Stopper** ($20, Dandelion, 888-548-1968).
* A **Caddie Pen** in the shape of a golf tee—red, green, or yellow ($10, Colorado Pen Company, 800-766-PENS).
* A **Scottish pewter flask**, shaped like a golf bag filled with clubs ($70, Dandelion, (888-548-1968).
* **Travel bag for golf bag and clubs**, Battenkill® leather and forest green canvas, fitted with wheels for easy transport ($148, Orvis, 800-541-3541).
* **Golf shoe bag filled with golfing goodies**: an adjustable cap, golf balls, score caddy, and a three-in-one divot tool ($59, 800-FLOWERS).
* **One dozen Spalding golf balls** imprinted with the golfer's photograph ($39, Celebration Fantastic, 800-235-3272).
* **Golf club drink dispenser**—a 48-ounce capacity cooler with a dispensing head that looks like a three wood, designed to fit into your golf bag ($39.95, Hammacher Schlemmer, 800-543-3366).
* **Golf putter tie bar** for him or **brooch for her**, 14k gold ($350, A.G.A. Correa & Son, 800-341-0788).
* The **Schmeckenbecker Putter**, equipped with a built-in compass to help you find your way out of the rough, a candle to illuminate the eighteenth hole after dark, a rabbit's foot for good luck, a level to help read the greens, and an air horn to silence or speed up other golfers ($39.95, Hammacher Schlemmer, 800-543-3366).
* **A lesson from a pro golfer.**
* **A tee-shirt that declares, GREENS ARE GOOD FOR YOU** ($19.50, Signals, 800-669-9696).
* **Electronic Golf Champion**, handheld video game ($16.95, Bits & Pieces, 800-JIGSAWS).
* **A week at golf camp**.

Christening and Baptism

Monogrammed or **personalized gifts** are appropriate, especially for a christening when the baby is receiving his name officially in the eyes of the church. Close family members may be able to provide a gown that has been passed down through the generations. If you don't have such an heirloom in your family, you can find a beautiful old **christening gown** at an antique store.

A great selection of religious gifts for those of the Catholic faith can be found at Catholic Supply of St. Louis (800-325-9026, or www.catholicsupply.com). For baptism, they offer a colorful **child's rosary** ($4.95) and a **Noah's ark nightlight** ($24.95).

Many of the ideas mentioned in chapter 4 are equally suitable as christening and baptism gifts (see pages 66–77).

First Communion

In the Catholic faith, first communion is a big event for children and their parents. For children receiving their first communion, a gift of religious significance is best: for Catholics, **a miraculous medal of a saint** whose name the boy bears, or **crystal** or **silver rosary beads** for a girl. A **gold cross pendant** could be worn by both. You'll find all of these, and a **First Communion Remembrance Frame** ($8.95), at Catholic Supply (see above). Gifts of **money, savings bonds**, or **shares of stock** are always appropriate.

Confirmation

Confirmation is a special ceremony where young people are admitted to full church membership. It is a sacrament and confers the gift of the Holy Spirit. A newly confirmed Episcopalian will appreciate the *Book of Common Prayer*; for a Catholic, a copy of *Lives of the Saints* is appropriate. Members of either religion can be given a **Bible** appropriate to his or her faith. Catholic Supply offers several different **crosses** and a **confirmation necklace** with the symbol of a dove in gold plate ($22). The best choice for a gift will be something of lasting value—a **watch**, a **fine pen**, a **gold cross**, or a **locket**—which they will associate with their confirmation in the years to come.

Bar and Bat Mitzvah

As they enter their teens, Jewish children are fortunate to have as an integral part of their culture this rite of passage, which signifies the most important occasion to date in their young lives. Gifts of lasting value, such as a **fine watch**, are most appropriate at this time. **Cash, checks**, or **savings bonds** are entirely fitting, as are **contributions to Jewish charities**. Money can be given in multiples of eighteen (or *chai*), which is considered lucky in the Jewish faith. You may also consider giving **music by Jewish composers** or **musicians, books about Jewish heroes** and heroines, **Jewish culture**, a **Kiddush cup**, religious **jewelry**, or a **medallion** made from an Israeli coin. In a catalog called The Source for Everything Jewish (800-426-2567) you'll find books and jewelry, as well as several personalized gifts specifically for the young celebrant, including two different **framed versions of Torah passages** ($75 and $125) and **Bar** and **Bat Mitzvah albums** ($35). There is a classic **Swiss Army knife**, rendered in blue with the Star of David ($22.95), and a sterling silver **Hebrew name ring** ($65).

8

Feel Better

Most people associate gift giving with holidays and special occasions, but there are times in our lives when a gift can also bring much needed cheer—and we all need cheering up sometimes. It might be a touch of the flu, an extended hospital stay, a recent divorce, or the death of someone close. In truth, some situations are so dreadful that our gift cannot possibly make someone feel better, but at least a gift can let someone know that we care.

Under the Weather

At the risk of being too obvious, I offer this suggestion to give to your friends who are under the weather: **chicken soup**. Everybody knows it's a surefire remedy—whether it's the steam that clears your head, or the love that goes into the preparation, or something intrinsic to the chicken itself—but how many people actually go to the trouble to make and deliver it? My own version appears below:

Sick Soup

For one serving, simmer two cups of chicken stock (recipe below; homemade is best), and add a little finely chopped clove of garlic, a pinch of cayenne pepper, the juice of half a lemon, one teaspoon grated fresh ginger. Serve steaming, sprinkled with some finely chopped parsley.

Chicken Stock

Cover a 3 to 4 pound roasting chicken with fresh spring water in an 8-quart stockpot. Add 10 sprigs of parsley; 2 sprigs of fresh thyme; 8 peppercorns; 1 onion stuck with 4 cloves; 2 stalks of celery, chopped; and 2 carrots, chopped. Bring to a boil, skim off the foam, and lower the heat to a gentle simmer. Continue to skim foam and fat off the surface. Cook for 2 hours. Strain.

Deliver a pot of soup by itself or include it in a **care package** with a funny video, comfort food like tapioca or polenta, some herbal tea, a box of tissues, Vick's VapoRub, and a hot water bottle.

Celestial Seasonings (800-2000-TEA) offers **Mama Bear's Cold Care Kit** ($24.98), which includes four different delicious medicinal teas, honey, three kinds of lozenges, two lip balms, and a wooden honey dipper. This is a great gift to give in anticipation of the cold season, or to someone who is already sniffling and sneezing.

Shop at a natural foods store for a supply of **E-mergen-C™**, **echinacea**, and **goldenseal herbal extract**, and some **fresh juices**. Tie the bag with a ribbon, and deliver.

Think about how to make life in bed more comfortable for a friend who is ill at home or hospitalized. Situations might include a pregnant friend on bed rest. Put together a collection of **body lotion**, **lip balm**, an engaging **suspense novel**, a stack of mail-order **catalogs**, a handful of **magazines**, a **notepad**, a **hot water bottle**, a soft **nightgown** or **pajamas**, and a good **pillow**. **Flannel sheets** are nice (Garnet Hill has the best, 800-622-6216). **A bed tray** is almost essential (you'll find a beautiful bed desk in Levenger, 800-544-0880, $129). You can give her a **bulletin board** for cards, cartoons, and medication schedules. Provide a **catered dinner**, if the patient's appetite is intact.

When you visit, take a box full of **paperback books**, new and used, covering a wide range of subject matter: biography, mystery, history, fiction.

Diamond Organics (888-ORGANIC) offers several healthy **Get Well Samplers**, designed for those recovering from an illness, or just plain down with a cold or flu. The **Cold & Fever Reliever Box** contains winter stew, mesclun salad mix, hearty sourdough bread, seasonal fruits, and a handwritten card with your personalized message ($42, including FedEx delivery). All the ingredients are organically grown and harvested to order. You can also send one of their charming **flower bouquets** (well-priced at $6.50 and $12.50), and they'll include it with no additional shipping charge.

A down-in-the-dumps friend might appreciate a **Sunshine Sampler** from Starbucks (800-STARBUC). A small wicker lunch box is filled with different coffees, in three cheerful half-pound bags.

I'm a firm believer in Norman Cousins's philosophy of laughter as a healer. With the caveat that "funny" is subjective, my recommendations in the video department: **vintage Gene Wilder**, *A Fish Called Wanda*, **the best of** *Saturday Night Live* (the early years), *Happy Gilmore*, *Dirty Rotten Scoundrels*, **Monty Python**, *Mr. Bean*, *Fawlty Towers*, *The Gods Must Be Crazy*, **The Marx Brothers**, *The Mouse That Roared*, *This Is Spinal Tap*, *Caddyshack*, *The Full Monty*, *Airplane*, *Naked Gun*. Think of what makes you laugh out loud, and wrap it up for a friend. Besides your local source for videos, you may want to consult the catalog of Video Yesteryear (800-243-0987), which features all the classics.

A **floral arrangement** is suitable to send someone who is hospitalized, unless the room is already overflowing with blooms, in which case it's thoughtful to **have the flowers delivered to the patient's home** later, for the recuperative period. You can also **plant a windowsill garden** with seeds, annuals, or bulbs; the patient can watch them grow while recuperating.

If someone you know is ill for an extended time, or recovering from a serious illness, give him or her a **dinner calendar**, filled in with the names of friends who will be delivering meals. Your gift is giving the

Gifts for the Perfect Stranger

* **Pay the bridge toll for the car behind you.**

* **Contribute to the holiday fund in your area**—they distribute directly to children in need.

* **Start a clothing drive for homeless people** in your community.

* **Visit a resident in a nursing home** in your community.

* **Donate to a food drive.**

* **Volunteer at a shelter for homeless people.**

* **Help an elderly person to cross the street.**

* **Merge courteously.**

* **Give to the blood bank.**

* **Help a young mother with small children**: offer to carry her bags or hold her child.

* **Let someone go ahead of you in the checkout line** at the grocery store.

patient a little unencumbered time to recover. Before you make the arrangements, find out about dietary restrictions and wishes, and on what days help is needed most. The same idea works for **child care** and **grocery shopping**. If the load is spread out, it won't tax anyone too much, and you'll find there are usually a lot of people who want to help, are wondering what they can do, and are just waiting to be asked.

For a Sick Child

A child who is hospitalized or at home in bed will enjoy a **tape recorder** or **Walkman**, and **books and music on tape or CD**, especially if he is not old enough to read or feeling up to it. Roald Dahl's stories are hilarious and appeal to a broad age range. A **book or magazine about nature**, **sports**, or **some special interest** allows the child to escape into another world.

Food treats like **cinnamon toast**, cut lengthwise into four "soldiers," **tapioca**, **fresh orange juice**, or a **special pastry** will perk up a sick little one. Preparing **hot cereals** and **comfort foods** can be our way to help in the healing, although it's important to keep the fare light.

The child will appreciate **drawing materials** or other **art supplies**, if she is not too sick to enjoy them. Younger children will like **crayons** and **coloring books**, an older child may prefer a **drawing pad** and a selection of **markers**, or a **black scratch board**. **Little puzzles** and **games** will also provide a needed diversion—being in bed all day is boring! Depending upon how ill the child is, consider going to a paint-your-own-ceramic store and purchasing a **mug or plate** for the child, along with an assortment of glazes. He can paint the piece, then you can take it away to be fired and bring it back to him a week later.

A sick child will appreciate a **summoning bell** for her bedside. I had one as a child, and it was part of the ritual of any illness, along with the **ginger ale** and the **Betsy McCall paper dolls** from *McCall's* magazine that my mother always provided. Any bell will do, so long as it can be heard throughout the house. You'll find a big bronze reception bell in the quirky catalog of the Lilliput Motor Co. ($45, 800-TIN TOYS).

If the illness is prolonged, a **small pet** (guinea pig, goldfish, or bird) might be a welcome distraction, but be sure to get parental approval in advance.

Finger puppets can provide hours of solo entertainment for a young one confined to bed. Fire Robin Puppets, in Vermont (800-235-5013), offers a whole menagerie of handmade, safe, machine-washable finger puppets including four different **bats**, a **hummingbird**, a **goldfish**, a splendid **dragonfly**, and many more, for $10 each.

Send a gigantic **Get Well banner** personalized with your own message (call Supergram at 800-3-BANNER).

Down in the Dumps

A person doesn't have to be ill to feel bad; we all get the blues at times, for various reasons big and small. Almost everybody feels better after a hot bath, so one of my favorite gifts for people in need of a little pick-me-up, myself included, is **Tub Tea**. This ingenious product is beautifully simple: giant tea bags, filled with fragrant herbs and flowers. Blends include: Everyday, Full Moon, Hot Afternoon, Cozy Weather, and Romance. All you have to do is pop the tea bag in the bath and let it brew. Three bags for $6, or a gift box of all the blends for $20, is available in New York at Ad Hoc Softwares, 212-925-2652, or at Restoration Hardware (call 800-762-1005 for the store nearest you).

If you know someone who is going through a rough spell, you can encourage her to rest and relax with lavender and bergamot **aromatherapy oils** ($3.95), a hardwood **massager** ($6.50), and a soothing **eye pillow** filled with flax seeds ($10.00). Available at the Body Shop (800-BODYSHOP).

Several people can band together to send a friend in need to a **retreat** or **restorative spa**. There are hundreds across the country, so word of mouth is probably the most reliable way to find one locally. What could be a more loving gesture?

Send **rose-colored glasses** to a friend whose viewpoint could use a little brightening. Have you ever looked through a pair? They really do make the world look wonderful. See your local optician or sunglasses store.

Just knowing that someone is thinking about him may help a friend to feel better, and a **little gift** is a nice way to show your thoughtfulness. If he has any sort of collection, find something to add to it, and send it along with **a note** and your sincere good wishes. For a faraway sick friend or relative, a **recorded message** is very welcome. It can be funny, silly, comforting, or serious. You can even record a bedtime story or fairy tale.

Nursing Home Gifts

The same gifts that are appropriate for a hospital patient may also apply to a friend or relative who is in a nursing home. A nursing home resident may be confined or have a considerable amount of freedom and mobility. In either case, however, there is often a feeling of isolation. You can make his or her living area seem more like home by bringing a special **pillowcase**, a **picture**, or fragrant **potpourri** for the bedside.

Most nursing home residents are inactive for a large part of the day, which tends to make them feel cold. Bring them a soft **knit throw** or a pair of **slippers**.

Older people sometimes have a sweet tooth. You can provide a bowl of **hard candies** or a tin of **homemade cookies** that they can enjoy and share with their friends.

Books or **books on tape** are a great way to pass the time, create new interests, and keep old hobbies alive (Audio Editions, 800-231-4261). A brief conversation may inform you about subjects and authors of special interest. **Music tapes of their old favorites** may also touch a chord. Give them **a tape cassette player** or **Walkman** so they can enjoy the books and music.

If they are able to get out, **take them to a movie, to get their hair done, on a shopping trip, or just a walk to town**. It'll be a great relief to have something new to look at.

Pampering gifts will mean a lot to nursing home residents. **Massage** can be very beneficial, if they are not too modest to enjoy it. A **manicure, pedicure**, or **facial** are other possibilities. You may be able to arrange for someone to come in to provide these services, if the resident is not able to get out easily.

And, of course, **the gift of your time**—for even a short visit—means more than anything.

Recent Divorce

Helping a friend cope with divorce calls for a great deal of sensitivity and often a willing ear. The situation requires a different response depending on your relationship to the person, and his or her state of mind. What many divorced people would like more than anything is to be able to continue their friendships, even though they are no longer a couple. An **invitation to a social event or dinner** will let them know you want to remain friends.

If you have a close friend who has recently divorced, you can **organize a shower** for him or her, but don't push the idea if he or she isn't enthusiastic. Stipulate in the invitation that gifts are to be replacements for things the spouse got in the split-up, or the gifts can be strictly the pick-me-up kind: a facial, a new lipstick, an inspirational book.

Offer to **pay for the first personal ad**.

I sent a good friend a **hot water bottle** with a note, "To help you keep warm in bed. I hope it's more reliable than your ex!" She thought it was funny, but obviously this wouldn't be appropriate for some people.

For the newly single man, consider **cooking classes**. It's a good place to meet nice people, and he'll learn a skill he may not have cultivated. I have a very civilized friend who actually gave this to her ex-husband.

Engraved stationery reflecting the new single status might provide a boost, but try to be reasonably certain that the current address will be a permanent one before you make this investment.

Bereavement

One of the most difficult situations any of us faces is how to comfort someone who has lost a loved one. The best approach is to come from the heart. One friend tells a story she calls "The Two Grapefruits." A member of a small Colorado mountain community died, and everyone visited the bereaved partner with bounteous gifts of food. One woman desperately wanted to show how much she cared, but she had nothing in the house to give as an offering; all she had were two grapefruits. So that is what she brought. It really doesn't matter what you bring, as long as you show up.

Gifts to Give Yourself

* **A day off**.

* **A luxurious bath**, with flower petals floating in the water.

* **A massage, facial, and manicure**.

* **A long walk in a beautiful place**.

* **Dinner by candlelight**, especially if you are alone.

* **Time off to pursue a passion**.

* **A new car**.

* **A gardenia** for your desk.

* **Time with friends**, doing what you want to do.

* **A whole stack of new CDs**, because all of us deserve to have more music in our lives.

* **Rent a vacation get-away**, **beach house**, or **cabin**, and invite friends for a slumber party to celebrate your birthday, or another momentous occasion.

* **Cashmere**.

Those mourning a death often just want to have **companionship**. Your gift is to be there and to listen. The bereaved person may not want to be alone, so visits in the days following a death are comforting. **Prepared meals** are a big help; the grieving person will be relieved of the burden of cooking, and he or she will have something to offer others who drop by.

Words of sorrow are the hardest to express, but it's important to try. You can start with a simple and truthful statement, "I am so sorry for your loss." **Cards** are appreciated, because they can be read over and over again. **Write down your memories** of the deceased, and share any **photographs** you may have.

Teenage friends of mine recently lost one of their own in a car accident. A few days after his death, they gathered and made a **collage** of his life, using their collective photographs and memories. Creating the collage gave them a chance to grieve and relive special moments they'd spent with him, and the boy's parents were touched by their gesture. The collage can also take the form of a **video**, if footage is available of sporting events, high school plays, parties, and graduation.

A few weeks to a few months after the death, your **continued calls and visits** will mean the most, when the services are over and others have resumed their lives.

There are many ways to memorialize someone who has passed. The time-honored method is to **give to a charity** or cause either specified or held dear by the deceased. You can also **plant a tree, create a garden, name a library shelf or park bench,** or **dedicate a room at a day care center** by purchasing the furnishings and toys.

In the Jewish tradition, **donations** in multiples of eighteen are given to honor a death because the Hebrew number eighteen spells *chai*, which means "life." Food may be taken to the family, but not gifts or flowers, and flowers are never sent to an Orthodox Jewish funeral.

Flowers are an acceptable remembrance in the Christian faith. **Mass cards**, whereby you make a donation to the church to ensure that the deceased will be remembered in a Mass, are common in the Catholic faith and can be brought to the wake or mailed to the family.

Special Days

You could say that every day is a special day for someone. I once saw a list of holidays, and there is some reason to celebrate virtually every day of the year. On such a list, you'll find the birthday of every U.S. President along with Florence Nightingale's birthday, Pine Tree Appreciation Day, Sister's Day, and Brother's Day, just to name a few. As fun as it would be to celebrate each of these days, most people simply don't have the time. But some holidays celebrate the people who are closest to us and provide us with an opportunity to show our appreciation.

Mother's Day

Mothers have been celebrated since time immemorial—after all, where would we be without them? The ancient Phrygians in Asia Minor held an annual festival to honor Cybele, the mother of all gods. The Greeks worshipped a similar goddess called Rhea. In Rome she was called the Magna Mater, or Great Mother. The Romans held a three-day celebration in the middle of March to honor her, called the Festival of Hilaria. With the coming of Christianity, the Roman festivities transmuted into a celebration to honor the Mother Church.

Mother's Day in America was first celebrated on May 12, 1907, and in 1914 President Woodrow Wilson declared the second Sunday in May a national holiday, Mother's Day. Credit goes to Anna Jarvis, who lobbied for the holiday for years, as a tribute to her own mother. It is now observed in more than forty countries around the world.

Mothers appreciate **a small gift or gesture initiated by the child**, more than an expensive present bought by someone else and given in the child's name. As a mother of three, I can say unequivocally that the best gifts I receive from my children on Mother's Day or any other day are the ones from the heart. My favorite vase was given to me by a young potter in the family, and I prize the moth-eaten rabbit's foot, the original poem, and memories of the homemade cake that the three of them encrusted with M&M's. These gifts mean more to me than fine jewels. Kids can share any of their special talents with mom on Mother's Day: **staging a play**, a **poetry reading**, a **musical recital**, or a **tap dancing performance**.

Dad, or a friend of the mother's, can help younger children to plan in advance and think about how to celebrate the day. One of our most important jobs as parents is to teach our children how to celebrate themselves and others by helping them establish traditions and rituals.

Mothers can always use a little pampering, and this is a good day to do it. Begin with **breakfast in bed**, including fresh-squeezed orange juice, a tiny bouquet of flowers, and her favorite newspaper. She'll love you for it, even if you burn the toast. While she's enjoying breakfast, ask her what she would like to do for the rest of the day.

What do mothers really want? Often, the mother of small children wants nothing so much as a little time to herself! A thoughtful dad will take the kids out for a few hours, maybe to hatch a Mother's Day surprise for her, while mom has some much-needed time alone. Later in the day it can be one big happy family again and mom will enjoy it all the more because she'll be refreshed.

A thoughtful gift for any mother is a gift certificate to a **day spa**. Their services can include everything from paraffin manicures and pedicures, facials and makeup application, to honey milk or herbal body wraps and deep muscle therapy massage. Some even provide transportation to and from via limousine.

She'll be delighted with a **basket of bath and body products**:

Gifts Kids Can Give

* **A certificate to wash and vacuum mom or dad's car**.

* **Breakfast in bed for the folks** (or a sibling!).

* **Baby-sitting coupons**.

* **A photo of yourself**, framed is nice.

* **A picture you have drawn**.

* **A poem you have penned**.

* **A book you have written and illustrated**. I was given one called *I'm a Dog, Not a Frog*, a series of verses about the family Golden retriever, Tucker, written by my son with only a little creative support from his dad. It's a treasure I'll have long after the store-bought stuff is forgotten.

* **Anything you have made yourself**: handprints cast in plaster, cookies, clay sculpture, sand candles, an illustrated calendar.

* **Fun food**, especially something quirky that the gift recipient has a passion for: anchovies, licorice, mangoes.

* **Take your mom or dad out to lunch**.

imported soap, a natural sponge, bath salts, a loofah, pumice stone, facial mask, along with a candle and a CD of lullabies, or a good book to encourage lingering in the tub.

Another great way to pamper mom on Mother's Day and all year long: the **Bath-of-the-Month Club** (800-406-BATH). They'll send a start-up kit ($29.95 plus shipping and handling), including Fango Mud Bath powder, imported from the spa at Abano Terme, Italy, one pound of Sarvar Sea Salts with French organic peppermint imported from Hungary, and a 4-ounce bottle of Eucalyptus Oil Bath Therapy. Then, for an additional $9 per month, mom receives two to four spa products: Rain and Bath Shower Gel, Tension Relief Foot and Body Soak, Mustard Rub. That way, she can have the spa experience at home whenever she likes.

Celestial Seasonings (800-2000-TEA) offers an **Herbal Spa Crate** ($29.98), which includes Tension Tamer Tea, Tub Tea, a wooden massager, eight tea bags to soothe the eyes, a eucalyptus candle, and a rubber ducky.

I'm honored that my boys are willing to give me the **gift of their time** on Mother's Day, and I usually request that we take a **family hike**. When I told my sons I was glad they were old enough to keep up with us on a hike, one of them said, "I'm glad you're still young enough to keep up with us!" So, while we can all share this outdoor time together, I cherish it. After the hike my husband and the boys **prepare a wonderful dinner**, while I relax in the bath with **a glass of champagne.**

If mom has the time in her schedule and likes to cook, give her a gift certificate for **cooking lessons**. A class on desserts is especially fun because making desserts is an extravagance she might not otherwise take time for. This is one of those gifts from which the whole family will reap the incidental rewards.

Another thing mothers cannot get enough of is **photographs of their kids**, particularly if the children are together in the shot and appear to be relatively harmonious. If they're framed, it's even better because moms like to show off their families. Start a Mother's Day tradition by making an informal annual **portrait of mother and offspring**.

For chocolate-loving moms, Godiva always has a special **Mother's Day box**, stuffed with chocolates and truffles and tied up with a bow. Shop in one of their 150 boutiques, or call 800-9-GODIVA.

Encourage the kids to **make a video** for Mother's Day. This may require a little adult help, but the creative direction can come from the children. It can be filmed and edited ahead of time, or be a chronicle of the day itself.

A beautiful Mother's Day book to consider: *Mothers and Sons* by Mariane Ruth Cook ($22.95, Chronicle Books). Give it to your mom, along with a photo of the two of you.

For an extra-special Mother's Day gift, give her a **mother's ring**, a gold band set with birthstones of each of her children. Call local jewelry stores; price varies depending on the size and number of stones. Or you can give her a collection of **miniature ½" sterling silver birthstone rings**, one for each child, to be worn on a sterling silver chain around her neck (rings, $20 each; chain, $12, Signals, the catalog of public radio, 800-669-9696).

Please don't forget stepmothers. Particularly if they are of the live-in variety, they deserve a lot of credit on this day, and other days. One friend who is a stepmom said she really felt like part of the family when her teenage stepson presented her with a **paper crown** on Mother's Day. The following year, he gave her a **scepter** with a star on the end, and the third year, a giant-sized **ring**. Queen for a Day! She can hardly wait to see what he'll dream up for the next installment.

Father's Day

Father's Day had its beginnings as an American holiday on June 10, 1910. The idea for the holiday was spearheaded by a woman named Mrs. John B. Dodd, who had a special appreciation for fathers because she was raised along with five siblings by her widowed father. It wasn't until 1966 that it was declared a national holiday by presidential proclamation.

This is a day to indulge dad, so if he wants to go to the **ball game** or go **fishing**, let him have his way! You know all the usual dad's day gifts: **ties** (check out the Jerry Garcia line) and **barbecue equipment** (I love the Weber Charcoal Grill with the gas starter and built-in bin to store briquettes, $425 from Frontgate, 800-626-6488). But don't be afraid to entertain new ideas.

Has he secretly always wished he could learn to fly? Let him—in a **MiG-29**. He'll take off from the Zhukovski air base near Moscow, with a Russian test pilot at the controls, and experience a thirty-minute joy ride with speeds up to Mach 2.1. The package includes ground and air instruction and five days of fun in Moscow. At $10,250, it's a little pricier than your local amusement park, but a lot more fun! Call Fly with Us, 800-335-9538. Maybe throw in a copy of Tom Wolfe's *The Right Stuff* ($7.50, Bantam Books) for his inflight entertainment.

A fine writing instrument is always in style. One of the best: a **Mont Blanc Le Grand Fountain Pen** with a 14K gold nib and platinum inlay. The engraved "4810" will remind him of the height, in meters, of Mont Blanc. (Levenger, 800-544-0880, or fine stationers, about $300)

Restoration Hardware (call 800-762-1005 to find out the store nearest you) is full of great gifts for dad. Their best-selling *Pocket Ref* ($9.95), described as "almost a nerd in your pocket," is filled with fascinating factoids you never knew you needed to know, like building material specs or the density of butter, feathers, and lead; Dad will love it. This terrific more-than-a-hardware store also sells a **60' leather tape measure** with a cloth tape ($15) that reels in, like the kind surveyors used to have.

If he's a beer drinker, give him a **sampling of microbrewery beers**, including two bottles each from six different breweries, with information about the selections. Choose from either Pale Ale or Lager ($39 from Celebration Fantastic, 800-235-3272, or shop locally). Pair the sampler with *The Beer Essentials* by F. Paul Pacult ($14.95, Hyperion), the ultimate consumer's handbook to the world's best beers.

And while he's watching Monday Night Football, he can pop his favorite brew into an elegant, **silverplate cold drink holder** ($15 from Dandelion, 888-548-1968). Add his monogram to make it even more stylish. Your sports fanatic will also love **season tickets** to watch his favorite team, or a **skybox** for the big game.

Sons or daughters can **invite dad for a special date**, à deux. This will mean so much, especially if the two of you are not often alone together. Go to **dinner**, a **ball game**, the **theater**, or a **museum**. If dad is the outdoorsy type wrap up a small piece of camping equipment, like a **tiny espresso machine** for backpackers, along with an invitation to go on a **camping trip** with you. One of my fondest memories of my father is going camping, just the two of us, when I was ten. You can do the same sort of thing for a **fishing trip**—the point is to have fun together.

Gifts for the World's Greatest Fisherman

* A **leather photo album** embossed with "Famous Fishing Trips" (Exposures, 800-222-4947).
* **The Fly of the Month Club**—Three classic, hand-tied freshwater flies delivered monthly, along with a written history of each pattern, beautifully presented with an onionskin overlay. Call Fishing Enthusiast (six months, $69.95; full year, $129.95), 800-597-0634.
* **Fly fishing lessons**, 2½ days, $395 (call Orvis, 800-541-3541, for details).
* **Chocolate Fishing Tackle**: milk chocolate reel, knife and lure, white chocolate bobber, dark chocolate pliers, and a bag of jelly worms. ($17.98, The Lighter Side, 941-747-2356).
* **Fish and Fly Ties** ($19 each from Orvis, 800-541-3541).
* **Fishing mouse pad** ($18, Whispering Pines, 800-836-4662).
* **Fisherman's flannel boxers**, covered with fly patterns ($16 at Orvis, 800-541-3541).
* **"WOMEN WANT ME, FISH FEAR ME" tee-shirt** ($19.50 from Wireless, 800-669-9999).
* **A gift certificate to the local fish market**, just in case he doesn't catch anything.
* **Cast-iron, painted fish bottle opener** ($10, Whispering Pines, 800-836-4662).
* **Fly fishing trip on the Middle Fork of Oregon's Rogue River** ($1,150 for five days, through the Echo Wilderness Company, 800-652-ECHO, details on the web at www.echotrips.com).
* **Fishing Sweets**, a colorfully painted tin of lemon drops from England ($4, Dandelion, 888-548-1968).

Would dad love a new **Porsche Boxster?** Give him a remote-control 1:12 scale model of one. It includes ergonomic bucket seats and a detailed driver's side console but travels only 12 mph, somewhat slower than the real thing ($69.95 from Hammacher Schlemmer, 800-543-3366).

A wooden **picture frame**, inscribed with gentle thoughts about dad, would look nice on any father's desk, particularly with your photograph inside ($28, Colorado Pen Company, 800-766-PENS).

If dad is a cigar aficionado, consider the following:

* A subscription to **Cigar Aficionado** (800-992-2442)
* A box of **Carmine Thrifties**, Francis Ford Coppola's favorite cigars for everyday smoking. Mr. Coppola has these Italian workingman's cigars imported from Italy and named for his father (a box of ten, $3.79, available only from Niebaum-Coppola Estate Winery, 707-968-1135).
* **A cigar box filled with stationery made from the byproducts of tobacco harvesting** in Latin America ($25, Colorado Pen Company, 800-766-PENS).
* A **Cohiba ashtray** ($45, Niebaum-Coppola Estate Winery, 707-968-1135)
* A **black leather travel humidor**, lined in seasoned mahogany ($295, Alfred Dunhill 800-860-8362)
* **A sleek, silverplate cigar lighter**, patented in 1928 and available only at Dunhill (800-860-8362)
* **A mahogany box filled with twenty-five Macanudos**, handmade in Jamaica ($110, Dunhill, 800-860-8362)
* **A box of ten Dunhill Miniature cigars** ($9, Dunhill, 800-860-8362)
* **Father's Day Cigar Box**—A great looking keepsake box with a hinged lid, filled with a dozen cigars the whole family can enjoy because they're made of solid milk chocolate ($35, Godiva, 800-9-GODIVA).
* **A silk cigar tie** ($33, Colorado Pen Company, 800-766-PENS)
* **Cigar cuff links** from Asprey ($200, 212-688-1811)

Father's Day is the second biggest holiday of the year for booksellers, second only to Christmas. If dad is a true bibliophile, look at the collection of finely-bound and antiquarian signed **first editions** at Asprey, or call for their *Connoisseur's Book Catalog* (212-688-1811). A gilt-edged, moroccan-bound first edition of *The Great Gatsby* is $2,500. Chances are, he'll appreciate just as much a volume you pick up at a library sale or choose for him from a secondhand bookstore ($.50 and up).

If your dad is a reader and a fisherman, you're in luck, because there must be 5,000 **books about fishing**. Choose one, wrap it up in newspaper ("fish wrap"), tie it with fishing line, and pin a hand-tied fly to the package. (See Gifts for the World's Greatest Fisherman, page 150, for more suggestions.)

Ask dad what his fantasy gift is and he just might say, **"A Harley."** While a new "hog" might not be in his future or your budget, maybe you can handle a **Harley belt buckle** ($48), **tee-shirt** ($20), or **business card case** ($29). Check out the possibilities in the Harley-Davidson catalog, which you can receive by calling one of their stores, or order through their website at www.harley-davidson.com.

Father's Day goes hand-in-hand with barbecue season. If the dad in your life is handy at the grill, consider something other than a new apron this year. Perhaps a **Steak Sampler** from Balducci's (800-BAL-DUCCI), which contains blue-ribbon filet mignons, rib-eye, and strip loin steaks. He can have a steak-tasting party, and with any luck, you'll be invited. Or get him a gift pack of five different award-winning **barbecue sauces** from around the country (call 800-SAUCES-1).

What about an **all-in-one remote control** that allows dad to command his entire electronic realm—TV, VCR, and CD player—up to eight applications at once? Mitsubishi makes this amazing gadget, and it sells for around $130 at fine audio stores. Dad will never again have to waste his time looking for the right remote control—this is it.

Guys love their cars, so give dad a **grooming kit** for his: a bucket filled with wax, a chamois cloth, Armor-all, a quart of oil, and a certificate for one free wash—a service you will personally render. Or choose the nifty **Roadside Safety Kit** from Restoration Hardware, complete with flares, flashlight, and safety triangle ($25, 800-762-1005).

Ten Last-Minute Father's Day Gifts He'll Love

1. **Tickets to a baseball game!** If you're lucky enough to live near a metropolitan area, take him to the Big League. Otherwise, minors, college, high school, or even Little League games will do nicely. And don't forget the hot dogs.
2. **Detail his car, inside and out.**
3. Has your dad always wanted a Ferrari? Give him one—for an afternoon, that is. **Dream car rentals** are available in most major cities. Imagine tossing him the keys . . .
4. **A new fly-fishing rod** ($105 and up) and lessons from Orvis (800-541-3541). They have five schools around the country and 2½-day classes are $395. Orvis is *the* source for vest, waders, and all manner of fishing gear.
5. Go to your local hardware store and select a **new barbecue grill and long-handled tools, a mitt,** and **an apron** to go with it.
6. **Put together a sampler of microbrewery beers** from the grocery or liquor store.
7. Give him a **gift certificate for lattes** at his favorite coffee bar.
8. **Make him breakfast in bed.**
9. Is dad a Gadget Guy? How about a **key organizer with a built-in minilight and clock** ($39.95) from the Sharper Image. Head for the mall, call them at 800-344-4444, or shop on-line at www.sharperimage.com.
10. **Send him food!** My father is still talking about the live crab and sourdough bread I shopped for locally and FedExed to his desert home. If you live far away from your dad, what's available in your area that he would love?

If your father has arrived at that stage of life when he needs to wear reading glasses, take the sting out by giving him a spiffy aluminum **eyeglass case** in the shape of a sports car ($10, Dandelion 888-548-1968).

Grandparents' Day

Grandparents' Day was first proposed in West Virginia in 1973 by a woman named Marian McQuade. In 1978, the U.S. Senate passed a bill declaring the first Sunday after Labor Day as National Grandparents' Day.

There is a lovely book, ***Little Things Mean a Lot: Creating Happy Memories with Your Grandchildren*** by Susan Newman ($14, Crown Publishing), absolutely filled with ideas to turn every grandparent into a "great" grandparent: "Add a morning, afternoon, or after-dinner walk with your grandchild to your visiting routine," or "Introduce your grandchild to fishing. Waiting for the bait to be taken is a good time to talk." If the grandparents in your life are active and involved with their grandchildren, this is a book they'll treasure. I bought one to save for when I become a grandmother.

Grandparents' Day is a good time to **telephone** or **write** to grandparents, and renew those family ties that seem increasingly tenuous in our society. You could even surprise them with a good, old-fashioned **telegram** (Western Union, 800-325-6000).

It is also an opportunity to send recent **photos** of your family. Family photos are almost impossible to overdo, and grandparents love to marvel at the changes. You can send a **photo album** and fill the first few pages with recent family snapshots with a pledge to send updates throughout the year. Give them a copy of the home **video** you made for Mother's Day; they'll be your most enthusiastic audience.

Have a **custom calendar** made from photos of the grandkids or family snapshots. These cost about $25 at local photography or printing shops and for an extra $10 can include your personal holiday; all the family birthdays, for example. If the grandparents are card players, you can have **playing cards** made with the kids' photos or artwork reproduced on a 52-card deck ($39.95, Exposures, 800-222-4947).

Whether or not grandma bakes, she'll love receiving **handprint cookie cutters** from each of her grandchildren. Send a tracing of your child's hand, and in three to four weeks you'll receive a heavy gauge aluminum cookie cutter made to size and engraved with the child's name, age, and an inscription of up to six words. Available for $15 from Cookie Cutters by Karen, 888-476-4525.

Another gift that requires a little advance planning is a **jigsaw puzzle** made from a photograph of your child or children. Grandparents can assemble the puzzle, then glue it in place and display it. You can order this through The Lighter Side (941-747-2356).

Kid art of all kinds will never find a more appreciative audience than the grandparents. Frame a **finger painting**, or make a **plaster cast hand or footprint**, and let the child paint it.

What better day than Grandparents' Day to give him a **grandfather clock**? And for her, a **ring with the grandchildren's birthstones**. This could be a gift from the whole family and include several stones.

Another his-and-hers idea: an **autograph of his favorite baseball hero** for Grandpa, and for Grandma, a **film star signature**.

Grandmother's Treasures by beloved author Lois Wyse (Crown Publishing, $18) is a keepsake designed to be handed down from generation to generation. This is a place for recording memories, and there are pockets in which to save clippings, letters, and photos.

You can let your grandparents know how much their family stories mean to you by giving them a copy of the book, ***Legacy: a Step-by-Step Guide to Writing a Personal History*** by Linda Spence ($14.95, Swallow Press), which will encourage them to write down their personal history for future generations.

Two books that would be especially appropriate for a child to give a grandparent are ***Grandfather Remembers*** and ***Grandmother Remembers*** by Judith Levy ($15.95, Stewart Tabori and Chang). There is space to fill in the family tree and memories of childhood, after which the grandparent can make a gift of the book back to the child. This truly embodies the notion of a gift as something that should be passed on.

Mothers and grandmothers will be pleased with a personal accessory like a piece of **jewelry** or a **silk scarf**. Among the best places to shop for consistently tasteful women's accessories are the museum shop catalogs. If you don't quite trust your own taste, you'll be safe with their selections. My favorites: Metropolitan Museum of Art (800-662-3397), The Museum of Modern Art (800-793-3167), and The Art Institute of Chicago (800-621-9337).

10

On the Job

Most of us spend a large part of our waking hours in an office, working and talking to the same people every day. The relationships that we develop at work are completely different from those we form with family and loved ones, but, nevertheless, they are very important to us.

Occasions for giving gifts at the office are frequent. Examples include co-worker's birthdays and weddings, promotions, departures, achievements, or simply in-office celebrations of important holidays. Of course, there is also the matter of giving gifts to clients and customers, which typically happens only at holidays such as Christmas.

One big difference between giving gifts at the office and giving gifts to friends and relatives is that the relationships we form at work are often characterized by rank—in other words who works for whom. Gift giving at the office is further complicated by corporate culture and politics. In some companies, lavish spending is the rule at the executive level. On the other hand, it is generally considered inappropriate by the etiquette experts to give your boss a gift, unless it is a small token like a plate of Christmas cookies. This depends a great deal upon the size of the company. Smaller companies are typically much more informal and relaxed about the traditional rules of etiquette. If you are new to a company, ask a co-worker to fill you in on the protocol. And, if the relationship transcends that of boss and employee, and you are friends outside of work, then regard the gift decision as you would for any friend.

For the Boss

Bosses are people, too. They have birthdays and celebrate holidays just like everyone else. What you give him or her for a birthday or Christmas depends largely on how close you are, personally and professionally.

A secretary who may be personally close to the boss and the boss's family will certainly want to give a gift to the boss. An appropriate choice might be a **basket filled with different foods** the family will enjoy, or a **board game**. It should not be too personal or extravagant, as this might prove embarrassing for the boss.

For others, an appropriate gift for the boss might be a **book** related to a business or personal interest. If your boss has an interest you are aware of—or perhaps even share—give a present you know he or she will appreciate, such as a **bottle of wine, golf balls**, or **tickets to a game, play, or concert**.

From the Corner Office

If you are an executive and have a number of people on your gift list, you might designate an assistant as your gift buyer, or even hire an outside service to handle it. One such company, California-based Custom Specialtees (415-551-9700), handles corporate gifts for Fortune 500 companies across the country, as well as smaller projects such as custom holiday gift shopping for celebrity clients. They have sources for everything from coffee mugs to silk sleepwear and baseball jackets, which can be personalized with logos or monograms. They'll take care of everything, right down to a custom wrap, and work with your budget and schedule.

Remember, gift buying takes a lot of time, so you may want to delegate. If you decide to go this route, be sure your gift buyer is briefed about the tastes and interests of your gift recipients as well as the price ranges you are looking for, so the selections will reflect your personal touch. A carefully chosen, beautifully wrapped package accompanied by a handwritten note will be much more meaningful than one that feels obligatory, regardless of the value.

If you've decided to give gifts, you will probably want to select more generous presents for your colleagues in the business community, as well as your board of directors. A gift of lesser value is in order for senior staff members, particularly if bonuses are given. Look to Asprey's (212-688-1811) Fun and Games department for impeccable executive toys: a **green leather dominoes set** ($325), a **purple leather poker dice set** ($65), a **sterling silver yo-yo** ($115), a **black-and-white leather chess set with wooden pieces** ($1495), or, my favorite, a **leather tic-tac-toe game** ($85). Asprey also has a fine **red calf leather and brass desk set** ($975), including blotter, pencil holder, memorandum paper holder, and bookends. You'll find a classic **hand-blown hourglass** gimbaled in a solid brass frame ($59.95) at the Mind's Eye (800-949-3333).

Your clients from other parts of the country or the world might appreciate a **gift basket of local foods**: New York specialties like bagels and egg cream, or a live crab, sourdough bread, and a Napa Valley wine from San Francisco.

A gift for your personal secretary or administrative assistant should be a reflection of their time of service. If they've been part of the team for several years, they should receive a bonus commensurate with any other key employee. For a gift they'll continue to enjoy all year, select a **beautiful vase** and have a **single flower or floral arrangement delivered weekly.**

If you manage a department or work with a small group of employees, hire a **massage therapist** who will come to your office and give fifteen-minute head, neck, and shoulder rubs to all interested employees. Some companies provide this as a regular perquisite, once a month; others offer it as a bonus at stressful times of the year.

If you are buying the same gift for several employees, it is a challenge to choose something that will satisfy the needs and tastes of a variety of people. Other possibilities besides the tried-and-true **Christmas turkey**: a **Christmas tree**, a **holiday wreath**, or a **large box of** boughs and candles, two or three different **coffee table books** to suit varied interests, a **leather mouse pad** ($25) or **monogrammed leather letter pad** ($95) with room for a pad of paper, ID, business cards, and pen (Colorado Pen Co., 800-766-PENS). For many occasions, a **small box of candy** is the ideal gift.

Save Time, Shop On-line

In these days of downsizing and right sizing, productivity is always an issue. A good way to save time doing your office gift shopping is to do it on-line. Check out the site of Virtual Vineyards (www.virtual vineyards.com). VV has several **monthly wine programs**, including all red, all white, or a mix: two bottles, four bottles, or six bottles monthly. One of their popular wine samplers is called, **"99 Dollars of Wine on the Wall,"** in which you receive an assorted case of their lower priced finds. There are also dozens of **specialty foods** at this site, including olive oil and estate grown coffees. VV is a good bet for **gift baskets**, too. If there are people you send gifts to on a regular basis, Virtual Vineyards will save their addresses on their "Friends List." Since they're on-line, they're able to react quickly to the marketplace, and their stock changes constantly.

For ordering **books** on-line, it's hard to beat Amazon.com at www.amazon.com. There, you'll find books for everyone on your corporate and office shopping list. You can search for titles by author or subject and quickly find exactly what you're looking for.

For Your Clients and Customers

Companies give gifts to thank their customers and clients, to build closer relationships, and as expressions of thanks for referrals. You can give clients and customers **gifts with your company logo**, providing it is small and discreet. Increasingly, logos are being seen for what they are—advertising—and people outside your organization may not be interested in promoting your name.

If there is any chance that your gift may be misinterpreted, a gracious letter may be a better choice. Or, instead of sending a gift to clients, you may want to give a **charitable contribution** in their name and send them a card to let them know.

Secret Santa and Other Office Traditions

Employees exchanging gifts with one another should try to be low-key about it to avoid bad feelings. In some companies, names are drawn and a spending limit is set. If everyone is participating in a gift exchange it can be an opportunity for a little lighthearted fun.

As any veteran of corporate America knows, the office may be so filled with Christmas spirit that the productivity level dips to near zero. Speaking of low productivity, this book will practically guarantee it: *How to Draw a Radish and Other Fun Things to Do at Work* by Joy Sikorski ($15.95, Chronicle Books). It's filled with all kinds of possibilities for what to do at your desk besides work.

A few more inspirational titles to give your colleagues: The *I Hate My Job Handbook: How to Deal with Hell at Work* by Ellen Tien and Valerie Frankel ($10, Fawcett Books), and *Shakespeare's Insults for the Office* by Wayne F. Hill and Cynthia J. Ottchen ($12.50, Clarkson Potter).

Dilbert, that poster boy of modern office life, is manifested in a daily **desk calendar**, and paired with his pals on a **colorful tie with snappy matching suspenders**. Or you can get a **Dilbert Mask**, complete with bendable necktie, and dare one of your comical colleagues to don it for the next staff meeting (The Lighter Side, 941-747-2356).

A small tin of elegantly simple, round **French paper clips** from Kate's Paperie (800-809-9880) are eminently appropriate for office gift-giving, and, at $5, totally affordable. A tiny **monogrammed black calfskin envelope** for business cards ($24.50, Eximious, 800-221-9464) might be just the thing for your boss or a co-worker.

Rather than worry about finding individual gifts for your office mates, you can order an **Office Goody Basket** ($108 from 911 Gifts, on the web at www.911gifts.com), an enormous thing filled with chips, salsa, gouda cheese, crackers, chocolate chip cookies, chocolate-covered Oreos, graham dunks, chocolate popcorn, jelly beans, almonds, pretzels, and chocolate truffles—in other words, something for everyone.

If one of your colleagues is forever doodling, you can covertly confiscate some of the more noteworthy examples of her art and have

Gifts the Boss
Can Give

∗   **Tickets** to the theater, symphony, ballet, sporting event, or concert.

∗   **Gift certificate to a restaurant.**

∗   **Gift basket of gourmet foods.**

∗   **A day of indulgence at a spa.**

∗   **Desk accessories** like pen and pencil sets, picture frames, clocks, date books.

∗   **Chocolates.**

∗   **Fruit, flower, wine, or coffee-of-the-month subscription.**

∗   **Magazine subscription.**

∗   **Desk fan or heater.**

∗   **Books.**

them turned into a very personal sort of **scratch pad** by your local print shop.

For the coffee lover in your office, an oversized **mug**, a **stainless steel Thermos**, or a plug-in **coffee warmer** are sure to be a hit. Coffee is at the center of the social scene in a lot of offices, so you're probably in safe territory here.

Make your own **gift certificates**: coupons to your nearby latte place, or four Friday lunches, for example.

Desk accessories are always in order. These can be of a serious nature—**blotters, bookends, calendars, picture frames**, an **electric pencil sharpener, pen and pencil sets**—or fun desk toys such as a **yo-yo**, a **miniature basketball hoop** for over the wastebasket, a set of **juggling balls**, a **dart board** (be careful here, you don't want to be responsible for impaling any of your co-workers), or small **dumbbells** ($3–6 at sports stores).

Gifts for the computer user include a **miniature battery-operated vacuum cleaner** with attachments to clean the keyboard ($20, 911 Gifts, on the web at www.911gifts.com), a mousepad, or personalized **screen saver**. How about a **milk chocolate P.C.** with your friend's name on the screen, or a **Hershey's logo Mouse Pad** that looks exactly like a giant bar of chocolate (Hershey's, 800-454-7737)? Or maybe a **laptop-toting gargoyle** to perch atop the computer (Signals, 800-669-9696).

Send "**E-greetings**" to all your wired office pals, so when they check their e-mail there will be personalized cards waiting for them, in addition to all the usual spam. At $.50 a pop, you can afford to be lavish. Choose from over 300 graphic images offered on the web by Greet Street (www.greetst.com).

If your cohort has a long daily commute, give him a **book on tape** or **Commuter Classics, Vol. I and II** (2 CDs, $24.95; two cassettes, $15.95, from Wireless, 800-669-9999), an exclusive compilation of classical music made with the commuter in mind.

Open for Business

The traditional gift given for the opening of a new office or practice is a **floral arrangement** or **plant**, and, while this is a lovely gesture, there are other options. You can send a **gift certificate to a local florist**, to be redeemed later, when the opening day bouquets have faded. If it is a professional office where music will be played, send a stack of suitable **CDs**. A framed **print** or **photograph**, especially one pertaining to the business at hand will be a lasting gift. If coffee and tea are served, you can arrange for different kinds of **beans** or **tea blends** to be sent each month for three, six, or twelve months. Call Starbucks, 800-STARBUC, or the Tea Club, 800-FULL-LEAF, to make arrangements.

National Secretary's Day

You can acknowledge this holiday in the usual ways: **take him or her to lunch**, or give the reliable gifts of **flowers** (1-800-FLOWERS) or **candy** (800-GODIVA); they will appreciate the acknowledgment. A few other ideas: **a day off; coupons for a month's worth of coffee** at the local hangout; a **personal parking place**; a **gift certificate for a day or half day at a spa**; a **gift certificate for a massage** (this may not be appropriate, depending on the person and your relationship); **dinner for two; a night at a bed and breakfast**. This is your chance to make your secretary feel special, so whatever you do, don't forget it—National Secretary's Day falls on Wednesday in the last full week of April.

Retirement

Retirement gatherings have been more frequent in recent years as many companies go through downsizing and reorganization. Whether the person has been terminated suddenly or is looking forward to a long-anticipated retirement, it is important to show your support and mark the occasion of departure. **Notes of remembrance** from colleagues (and students, if the retiree is a teacher) can be assembled into a scrapbook that chronicles the chapter just ended. Issue a **standing invitation** to the annual company party, so you don't have to make your final goodbyes. (See page 130 for more retirement gift suggestions.)

Gifts for the Office

* **Natural cherry desk accessories** to spiff up any office: pencil holder ($29.95), envelope holder ($29.95), bookshelf ($49.95), in-basket ($36.95), tape dispenser ($49.95, Levenger, 800-544-0880).

* **Leather mouse pad** (black or cognac, $25, Colorado Pen Company, 800-766-PENS).

* **German eraser stones** ($12.95, Levenger, 800-544-0880).

* **Severe weather screen saver**—allows you to while away the hours watching thunderstorms, tornadoes, and hurricanes, in the safety of your own office ($27, Wireless 800-669-9999).

* **Crocodile stapler in pewter** ($50, Colorado Pen Company, 800-766-PENS).

* **A keyboard vacuum**, complete with all the attachments for cleaning computers, fax machines, and cameras ($20, 911 Gifts on the web at www.911gifts.com).

* **A Swiss Caran d'Ache pen**, the same writing instrument Francis Ford Coppola uses to pen his screenplays (available in a host of fashion colors, $11, at Niebaum-Coppola Estate Winery, 707-968-1135).

11

Thank You

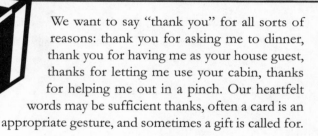

We want to say "thank you" for all sorts of reasons: thank you for asking me to dinner, thank you for having me as your house guest, thanks for letting me use your cabin, thanks for helping me out in a pinch. Our heartfelt words may be sufficient thanks, often a card is an appropriate gesture, and sometimes a gift is called for.

House Guest

As you strive to be the Perfect Guest, look at things from the Host's point of view and ask yourself what makes a Bad Guest: visits of more than three days; the guest who uses your phone to conduct his affairs for hours on end; the one who jumps in the shower and uses all the hot water just when everyone else in the house is getting ready for work or school and wants to shower, too; the guest who neither cooks nor buys groceries; the guest who keeps you up half the night. (She's on vacation, but you have a 7:00 meeting the next morning.) Then show your appreciation to your host by being a good guest—and give a thoughtful thank-you gift, too. That way, you will greatly improve your chances of being welcome next time.

Bring a gift for the host when you arrive, or send one after the visit, or both. It's nice to show up with a small gift of food and wine, and then to send something more substantial after your departure, particularly if your visit is for more than a few days. As a guest in their home, you will have an opportunity to see what your hosts need. I had house guests recently who returned home after a delightful visit and promptly sent a beautiful **bread knife**, along with a **gracious note** and **photographs** of our visit together. After struggling for several days with the loose handle of my old bread knife, they knew just exactly what to send me, and every morning when I slice my toast I think of them.

If you're staying with someone for more than overnight, a thoughtful way of giving back may be to **take the gang out to dinner or brunch** or, if your talents are up to it, **shop for and clean up after a great meal that you prepare** while your hosts visit with you and relax for a change. They'll definitely appreciate it.

Leave a **trail of gratitude** behind when you depart: a food treat hidden in the pantry, a "farewell" on the refrigerator, a note tucked under the pillow, a "thank you" message on the answering machine.

When you arrive home, send something that might be common in your part of the world, but which would be treasured in the place you've just visited. I sent a FedEx package to my folks with **two live crabs and a loaf of San Francisco sourdough**, available at my local grocery, but unobtainable where my parents live in Arizona. After another visit, they received a box filled with **baby vegetables and greens, a loaf of bread**, and **sausage** from my local farmer's market. It could be **Vermont maple syrup, regional honey**, a **locally brewed micro-beer**, or **indigenous art**. I have a California friend who received a big box filled with famously brilliant **autumn leaves** from New England—this was much more touching than anything the sender could go out and buy.

There are numerous companies that send gift baskets of food that are fitting gifts to say thanks for a great visit. One of the more unusual ones is Diamond Organics (888-ORGANIC). They feature organically grown baby salad greens, vegetables, herbs, and fruit, all picked to order and shipped via FedEx. Their gift assortments include the **Fruit and Goodie Basket**: Fuji and Granny Smith apples, Anjou and Bosc pears, Valencia and Navel oranges, and chocolate and nuts (all organic). They also offer the **Gourmet Greens & Vegetable Sampler**: a selection of specialty greens such as arugula, baby bok choi, and radicchio; specialty lettuces, fresh herbs, edible flowers; seasonal vegetables such as bunched baby carrots, baby leeks, tomatoes, baby zucchini, fresh peas, haricots verts, cucumber, and broccoli, with recipes included. They even have **organically grown flowers** that have all the charm of a homegrown bouquet and are several days fresher than what you're likely to find at the local florist. The flowers are priced very reasonably at $6.50 and $12.50, and can be included in a regular order with no extra delivery charge. In some parts of the country, it is still difficult to find a real loaf of bread; they have a beautiful assortment of twelve kinds of **organic bread** from a Northern California bakery, most in the $3–4 range. If your hosts are not among the fortunate few to live near a year-round farmer's market, one of these gifts will be an incomparable treat.

For those with a sweet tooth, consider an all-purpose **Thank You Basket** from Miss Grace Lemon Cake Company ($40, 800-FOR CAKE). It includes the original lemon cake in a signature tin, six each of the carrot walnut and chocolate fudge mini muffins, six chewy chocolate chip cookies, and an embossed THANK YOU coffee mug, all packed in a wicker basket tied with THANK YOU ribbon.

A **basket of specialty foods you assemble yourself** will strike a more personal chord. If the host has a predilection toward a particular cuisine, you have a theme to follow: Thai could include satay sauce, green curry, coconut milk, fresh ginger, and lemon grass; Italian might be sun-dried tomatoes, biscotti, fresh mozzarella, and your own roasted red peppers.

Send a chocoholic's idea of heaven: a **box made of chocolate**, filled with chocolates, with THANK YOU molded on the top. ($37, 1-800-FLOWERS). Sweet, simple, and to the point.

You can encourage your hard-working hostess to relax after your visit by sending a gift box of **Tub Tea**, oversized tea bags for the bath that contain lavender based blends of herbs and flowers ($20, Restoration Hardware, call 800-762-1005 to find the store nearest you). Or, send a box of **guest soap**; I love the Scottish Pure & Simple Citrus Sampler, $38 from Chambers, 800-334-9790.

Gifts for Your Child's Teacher and Coaches

* **A centerpiece of dried flowers.**

* **A silk scarf.**

* **A pin.**

* **A pen.**

* **Gift certificate for dinner.**

* **Gift ceritificate to a spa.**

* **A basket of assorted apples.**

* **A tie depicting the team sport.**

* **Tickets to the Big Game.**

* **A baseball, soccer ball, basketball, or football** signed by all the players.

* **A team picture** signed by all the players.

* **A letter jacket or warm-up jacket** in your team's colors with the coach's name embroidered on it.

Who'd have thought you could send a gift of **ice cream** through the mail? Out of a Flower, Inc. (800-743-4696) ships all over the country (five pint minimum), and this is not just any ice cream. Their ice creams and sorbets are made from edible flowers and fresh herbs, with all natural ingredients and no preservatives. Flavors include Peach and Champagne with Mint, Pear and Cinnamon Basil, Red Ginger and Red Port, and French Lavender. Maybe this is a thank-you gift you'll want to send ahead of time, so you can get in on the treat! In addition to their mail-order operation, they are sold at 125 stores, including Dean & Deluca and Whole Foods Markets.

Starbucks offers several samplers that make great gifts for coffee drinkers, and that describes most of us. You can say thank you with their **Popular Sampler** ($21.95), which includes 4 half-lb. bags of their favorite beans, ground or whole. I also like their **Hot Java Jazz Duo** ($19.95): a CD of jazz faves including Ella, plus a pound of Estate Java beans. To order, call 800-STARBUCS, or visit one of their 1,100 stores.

For something a little more conventional, peruse Balducci's catalog, or call them for suggestions (800-BALDUCCI). An apt choice would be the **Mille Grazie** ("A Thousand Thanks") **Basket**, filled with coffee, tea, chocolates and cookies and other sweet treats.

If you're lucky enough to be invited to a mountain cabin or a lakeside cottage, show your appreciation by contributing to their **sporting equipment** (croquet, badminton, a Frisbee), or give them a **deck of cards and some poker chips**, or a **board game** to liven up rainy afternoons. My favorites include: Scrabble, Clue, Monopoly, Trivial Pursuit, Balderdash, and Scattergories. Be a good guest and leave behind some **books** for their library, an essential part of any vacation home.

Dinner Guest

Part of being a good dinner guest is arriving when you're supposed to, and departing before your hosts begin to yawn, exchange glances, and look at their watches. If you've accepted an invitation to dinner, you are expected to stay for the evening and not cut out before the dessert course, unless you arranged this ahead of time with your host.

Flowers are a traditional way to say thank you for a dinner invitation.

It's perfectly appropriate to show up at the door with a bouquet, but it's even more thoughtful to send the flowers ahead of time, so your host doesn't need to scramble for a vase at a time when he probably has enough to do. Or have flowers sent the next day, after you've had a chance to see the color scheme and style of the home.

Or, instead of flowers, take along a favorite **plant for the garden**. A colorful flowering annual is great, but if it's a perennial, so much the better, as it will return year after year.

A dinner guest may bring a **bottle of wine** or **champagne**, tied with French wire ribbon or wrapped in a velvet bag. Anything homemade is literally priceless, be it **pesto, relish, jam,** or a **loaf of bread**. Taking a few minutes to wrap it makes it that much more special. The host may choose to save or serve your offering, but either way it will be appreciated.

A wood crate filled with **chocolate-dipped dried pears** from Manhattan Fruitier ($15, 800-841-5718) is an elegant little thank you to take to a special dinner, or you can send one of their spectacular **fruit baskets** ($50 and up) if you've been a house guest.

When you're attending a dinner party at the home of a friend, slip into the master bedroom and **leave chocolate truffles on the nightstand**, with a thank-you note. Your hosts will discover your surprise when they collapse into bed, after the last guest has departed.

New Yorkers have known about Sarabeth's for years—Sarabeth started a restaurant on the Upper West Side in the early eighties and soon became known for her baked goods and preserves. They're probably as close as you'll come to homemade, maybe better. Now you can order them for yourself, or send them to someone else. **Preserves** are sold singly ($15) or in gift sets of three ($36); I like the Rosy Cheeks (strawberry and apple), Billy's Blues (blueberry, blackberry, raspberry, and cranberry), and the Blood Orange Marmalade. Call 800-PRE-SERVE.

A collection of **chunky beeswax candles**, in various sizes, will be appreciated by almost anyone. These are widely available, but you'll find an especially great collection at Illuminations (800-CANDLES), whose stores and catalog are devoted exclusively to, what else?—candles.

When in Doubt

There is no gift that will please all the people all the time, but the following suggestions are good bets if you're stumped.

* **Books**. There is a book out there for just about everyone. From the steamy supermarket romance novel, to the luscious coffee table tome, there are books for all budgets and interests.
* **Music**. This gift can be given in the form of a hundred dollar bill and two hours at the record store, symphony or concert tickets, or a tape you record yourself.
* When in doubt, turn to Tiffany's (800-526-0649). The **silver Swiss Army knife** (plain, $110, or with a leaf pattern, $130), **silver screwball key ring** ($40), or one of their **silver pens** ($40–125) are all sterling, which should please almost anyone.
* **Photo frames**. Exposures (800-222-4947) has a great selection of fine quality frames, both playful and sophisticated.
* **Flowers**. Shop locally or at 1-800-FLOWERS, 24 hours a day, for seasonal and dried arrangements suitable for most people and most budgets.
* **Chocolate.**
* **Coffee.**
* **A stack of greeting cards**, blank or scripted, and **colorful stamps** tied up with a ribbon.
* **A bottle of fine wine.**
* **A gift basket** from Chelsea Market Baskets, 888-727-7887.

House-sitters, Dog-sitters, Baby-sitters

When you engage someone as a house-sitter or pet-sitter, the most fitting way to say thank you is with **cash**. The appropriate amount varies greatly, depending on where you live and the extent of the responsibilities involved. A fifteen-room mansion will cost you more than a one-bedroom cottage, and if your menagerie includes a dog, two cats, four fish, and ten chickens (as mine does), you'll need to pay your pet sitter more than you would for one gerbil. The compensation may also depend in part on the age of the person you engage and his or her relationship to you. A professional will expect more than your thirteen-year-old neighbor. A daily rate should be established before you leave, to avoid misunderstandings or hurt feelings. When you return, you can bring a small token gift, perhaps a **souvenir** or **food** from the place you've visited. If it's a friend doing you the favor, a **gift certificate to a restaurant** or a small gift may be more appropriate than cash.

Special Events

When you're invited to a special event, be it a party, the rodeo, or a basketball game, you can take photos of all the guests, then take the film to a speedy developer. Send a **small album filled with the party pictures**, along with your thank-you note to the hosts. Underwater and wide-angle disposable cameras can be invaluable in these situations. Photos create memories, so be the one to remember the camera.

12

Wrap It Up

Gift wrapping is almost as important as the gift itself. Receiving a present is so wonderful, in part, because of the ritual of untying and removing the bow, then carefully loosening each end of the decorative paper—or ripping it away, depending on your style—and then peeking into the box. One drawback to buying gifts on-line or by phone is that these stores often do not offer gift wrapping, or if they do, it is usually a box with a sticker on it, advertising the store. The thrill is a little bit diminished if your gift is contained in a corrugated cardboard shipping box and surrounded by plastic peanuts. Purchasing the gift is only part of the picture. Think of gift wrapping as the icing on the cake—it only helps to make your wonderful present even better. The way in which a gift is wrapped can reflect the personality of the giver or the receiver. I recently atttended a baby shower given for an art director by a group of graphic designers, and the gifts were too gorgeous to unwrap! One woman found a tiny antique French clothes hanger and swathed it in silk ribbon to show off the little outfit she'd selected. A beautiful presentation can make even the simplest gift memorable.

Tools of the Trade

Candy Spelling, wife of the Hollywood magnate, Aaron Spelling, takes the art of gift wrapping seriously. She resides in an enormous mansion in the Hollywood Hills, in which she has devoted an entire room to gift wrapping. In this chamber, she stores her wrapping resources including sheets and rolls of paper, ribbons, bags, boxes, and bows, and of course, scissors and tape.

You don't need a whole room for these supplies, but by all means, dedicate a very large drawer or a closet shelf to the task. A gift-wrapping station in your home office is even better. If space is limited, Hold Everything (800-421-2264) has a special box just for this purpose. This is where you'll store all that great gift wrap you stockpiled when it was half-price last January, along with wrapping staples, including parchment paper, gift bags, lunch bags, boxes, Chinese take-out cartons, colored tissue paper, organdy, curling and French wire ribbon, gold cord, notary seals, a hole punch, a glue gun, pinking shears, finger paints and paper, fabric paint tubes, and felt pens. You'll also accumulate miscellaneous decorative embellishments: ornaments, cookie cutters, charms, buttons, dried flowers, dried pomegranates and oranges, or orange slices, starfish, and pine cones, which may someday serve to turn an ordinary gift into something special.

Your gift wrap collection should include a variety of paper appropriate for different seasons and occasions, or if you want to simplify, you can choose one paper to be your signature gift wrap, like burnished gold tissue with raffia, or shiny white paper with silver ribbon. Tissue paper can be used alone, or layered over heavier paper. Keep waxed tissue paper on hand to wrap up homemade food items. Gift wrap can also include aluminum foil, brown parchment paper, old maps, the Sunday funnies, wallpaper, and fabric: silk, felt, or burlap.

The Japanese art of gift wrapping, called origata, embodies a complex set of rules regarding the relationship between the gift giver and the gift recipient, the occasion of the gift giving, the season of the year, and the gift itself. The components of Japanese wrapping: washi (handmade Japanese paper), mizuhiki cords, and furoshiki (cloth) make a wonderful gift in themselves, accompanied by small decorative additions like pine cones, leaves, and dried flowers, and perhaps a book on how to do it.

While some of the Japanese paper wrapping is very intricate and involves a lot of folds and flourishes, furoshiki ("fur-OHSH-key") wrapping is ridiculously easy to implement. A furoshiki is simply a square piece of cloth. The gift is placed diagonally on the fabric, you draw up opposite corners, and tie a knot. You can use any fabric, including a scarf or bandanna, and the wrapping becomes part of the gift. The important thing is that the fabric must tie nicely, so avoid stiff material. The Japanese favor cotton and silk; soft, washed linen works well also. Felissimo, that great New York store, sells an authentic Japanese furoshiki in seven shades and two sizes, small (18 inches square), $7.50, or large (27 inches square), $17 (800-565-6785). Even if you're all thumbs, your gift will look beautiful wrapped in this way.

Complimentary gift wrap usually means a box, a ribbon, and a sticker advertising the store. If you're lucky, the store may actually put your purchase in the box for you, although more often they will merely put the box in the bag with your gift and leave you to your own devices. Not so at Kate's Paperie in New York (800-809-9880). They have elevated the art of gift wrap to a new level, and whether you buy a $5 box of paper clips, or a $4,000 antique brush holder, they will wrap your gift for free, using some variation of the three-pleat Japanese style. Their staff of five gift wrappers (ten at Christmas) are trained in the Japanese tradition and will also do breathtaking and intricate custom wrapping, for a fee. The only drawback is your gift recipient will not want to open the beautiful package. New Yorkers take note: You don't have to buy your gift at Kate's to avail yourself of their extraordinary wrapping service. People shop all over the city and come in with shopping bags full of gifts to be wrapped. Price depends upon how elaborate you want to get. Be sure to give them plenty of time, especially during the busy holiday season.

Kate's also sells the components for great gift-wrapping: Florentine papers (six sheets, $22), iridescent marbled paper (six assorted colors, $19), handmade paper from Madagascar with ferns and flowers throughout (three sheets, $24), traditional Japanese cord (thirty yards, assorted colors, $17.50), and raffia in a ten-color assortment ($16). Tissue paper (200 sheets, $37.50), angel hair ($12), and cording (27 yards, $18) are all available in silver, copper, and gold metallic tones. I love the European shop paper, with a subtle straw-colored stripe and gloss surface that gives new meaning to the idea of kraft paper (two 33-foot rolls, $12).

Sometimes an economical approach to gift wrapping is necessary, especially around the holidays. At Christmastime or anytime, unroll a generous length of brown mailing paper, or white butcher paper, and decorate it with handprints, stencils, illustrations from magazine ads or greeting cards, or stamps made from cross-sections of fruits and vegetables. Kids love to do this, and the results can be beautiful. They can also paint either the paper or the package, once it's wrapped. Strips of fabric, cut with pinking shears, can be used for ribbon.

Simple wrapping can be embellished with a little special something tied to the package: a candy cane, a tree ornament, a cookie cutter, a doll or doll house furniture, a charm, a tiny bottle of Tabasco sauce, a fun pencil, a small flashlight—the possiblities are endless. It's even better if it relates to what is inside: a wooden spoon for a cooking gift, a roll of film for a photo album, seed packets on a gardener's gift, a bookmark tied onto a gift-wrapped book, or add a Christmas ornament to make a holiday gift a little bit special. A child's gift can be tied using a strip of stickers in lieu of more conventional ribbon.

Another idea is to wrap a gift in plain brown paper and decorate it with a paper chain of little people, or tie on some grasses, pods, feathers, or cones with raffia or twine. If you've got the time, you can really have fun with this, and the results can be elegant, funny, kitschy, or shabbily chic.

Road maps make a clever wrap for a bon voyage gift. Architectural blue line plans are good for gift paper, especially for housewarming presents. Photographic supplies, heavy matte black or black/white aluminum that comes in rolls can be used to sculpt odd-shaped packages, or make big bows. Not cheap, but very cool.

Because of their size or shape, some gifts can be a real challenge to wrap. For a large, odd-sized, or hard-to-wrap gift, use a galvanized trash can and crumple decorative tissue or the Sunday funnies to fill in the top. You can also use this approach for smaller gifts. Kids love this idea and so will you: wrap up a tiny gift in a huge box, and disguise it with rattling things like paper clips and dried beans, rolling things like marbles and baseballs, or heavy things, like bricks. If the gift is simply too big to wrap, like a bicycle, you can drape it with a strand of tiny white lights. If the gift comes in a very large box, you can paint the box with latex paint and a roller, rather than attempting to wrap it.

Some special gifts just don't lend themselves to wrapping, so you have to be creative. I gave my husband an Apple Macintosh computer when they first came out. The box was huge and I was afraid the size would give away the gift, so I hid the computer in a closet and tucked into his stocking, guess what? a Macintosh apple, with a note, "Think about it." My favorite all-time gift was a puppy; wrapped up under the Christmas tree were a box of dog biscuits, a leash, and a training book. If you're giving a gift of travel, you can wrap a guidebook. One friend gave his seventeen-year-old son a toy car, and when the son turned to make a face, dad tossed him the keys to the real car, waiting outside.

A gift of money can be presented in several fun ways in addition to the tried-and-true method of inserting a check or bills into a wallet. You can give a stem of orchids or lilies, and include the check or cash in the tiny gift envelope attached. Or put the check in a simple frame, which can be reused. Buy a Money Maze, a clear Plexiglas puzzle, and they'll have to figure out the trick before they can get to the cash (The Lighter Side, 941-747-2356). If the gift is earmarked for something specific, you can hint at it by the way you wrap it. Think miniature: if the money is for travel, tuck it into a Barbie suitcase, if it is for a down payment, put it inside a Lincoln Log house. Cash for kids can be cleverly disguised by pleating it, accordion-style, and tying it on to the tail of a kite. You can tuck a few real bills into a game of Monopoly, or put them inside a miniature safe ($14.95, The Mind's Eye, 800-949-3333). If you're giving a gift of stock certificates, gift wrap them in stock exchange newspaper. My husband gave me a blank check for new clothes and wrapped up a Barbie outfit hanging on a little pink plastic coat hanger, with little pink plastic high heels.

When you're overwhelmed by the sheer volume of gifts you have to wrap, consider hiring someone to deal with it. It's sort of like having your taxes done: You still have to be organized to some degree, in that each gift must be labeled as to who it is going to, but that's about it. Depending on who you hire, they may come with their own paper, tape, scissors, and ribbons. A skilled gift wrapper can manage fifteen to twenty gifts per hour—isn't it worth it? This is also a great surprise gift to give to a friend who is having trouble coping with the holiday madness.

Write to the Heart of the Matter

Your job is not complete once the present is purchased and wrapped. There is the matter of the gift card. It is, after all, the message that goes with the gift you are giving, and the presentation is incomplete without an expression of your sentiments. Not to put down the greeting-card industry, but I think it is best to write your own sentiment. Whether it be a simple, "Thanks!" or "To my favorite nephew," it'll mean more if it's written in your own hand. Your message should be simple and heartfelt, and if you are at a loss for words you can consult a book such as, *When Words Matter Most* by Robyn Freedman Spizman ($14, Crown Publishing), *Just a Note to Say . . .* by Florence Isaacs ($17, Clarkson Potter), or *Special Words for When You Don't Know What to Say* by Joyce Landorf Heatherley ($19.99, Ballantine Books).

Along with your closet full of gift-wrapping materials, you will want a good supply of gift and occasion cards. Keep an accordion file for your card collection, divided and labeled according to holiday or occasion—birthday, new baby, get well, anniversary, Christmas, Hanukkah, Easter, Valentine's Day—as well a section for blank cards, which are my favorite because they are appropriate for all sorts of occasions, and you get to make up the message. Shop for cards at your leisure, a few at a time, and keep the file well-stocked. That way you'll have cards available whenever you need them. The accordion file itself makes a great gift for someone else, too. Choose just a few cards in each category to start their collection, and include several fun stickers, some sealing wax, and a pen that writes in gold.

A card can be a gift in itself. Some are suitable for framing, and you can always tuck in cash, a letter, photos, recipes, rose petals. You can make your own cards using kids' drawings, photos, or last year's recycled Christmas cards, just cut off the greeting. Or you can print your own cards with the help of a Cardmaking Kit ($29.75, from the terrific art supply catalog of Daniel Smith, 800-426-6740), which includes two printmaking blocks; a linoleum cutter set and brayer; black, red, and gold ink; ten blank cards; and a gold pen.

And then there's the virtual card. You can send "E-greetings" to all your wired friends for only $.50 apiece. They're fun to receive! Choose from over 300 graphic images offered on the Web by Greet Street (www.greetst.com). This on-line company will also address, stamp, and send cards on your behalf in the old-fashioned manner, through the U.S. Postal Service, for $3.75.

Gifts by Category

Active Senior
* barbells, 25
* duffel bag for workout clothes, 25
* a fanny pack, 115
* a pedometer, 115
* membership to a gym, 115
* subscription to the opera, ballet, or symphony season, 44
* one week at Elderhostel, 128
* travel guidebooks, 128
* a subscription to *Travel & Leisure* magazine, 128
* gardening tools, 12
* cooking classes, 129
* two weeks with Outward Bound, 127
* outdoor games (badminton, smashball, croquet or volleyball), 110
* a garden tour of England, 12

Far-Away Friend
* special food from your hometown (New York bagels, Baltimore crab cakes, Philly cheese steaks, San Francisco sourdough, etc.), 5

* SEND-A SONG, 7
* recorded memories or songs on cassette, 30
* Bath-of-the-Month Club, 117
* a Sunshine sampler from Starbucks, 136
* Peach and Champagne with Mint ice cream through the mail, 170
* write her a long letter, 91
* a framed photograph of the two of you, 81
* airline bonus miles to bring him to visit you, 91
* a prepaid telephone calling card, 124
* stationery, 42
* surprise her with dinner delivered to her door, 27

Working Mom
* a calendar of special days, 3
* Menu of the Month, 44
* a pager, 23
* send a child to camp, 21
* flowers for her desk, 83
* manicure and pedicure, 75
* a laundry or cleaning service, 76
* a cashmere and silk robe, 90
* breakfast in bed, 26
* a few hours consultation with a professional personal organizer, 61
* Bath-of-the-Month Club, 117

The Commuter
* books on tape, 30
* vintage radio show tapes, 30
* Commuter Classics, 163
* a Walkman or Discman, 106
* travel neck pillow, 47
* membership to the Crossword Club, 118
* pager, 23
* the Roadside Safety Kit, 127
* a stormproof umbrella, 47

City Dweller

* apartment tool kit, 41
* subscription to the opera, ballet, or symphony season, 44
* the Ultimate Dust Pan, 63
* coco fiber welcome mat, 64
* Plant a windowsill garden with seeds, plants, or bulbs, 136

Sports Fan and Fitness Buff

* tickets to pro, semi-pro, or college sporting events, 18
* personalized wool stadium blanket, 43
* duffel bag for her workout gear, 25
* a cross-country ski trip, 90
* the latest at-home exercise equipment, 90
* bicycle helmet, 129
* a pedometer, 115
* a chin-up bar, 18
* a jump rope, 18
* send a message on the stadium's scoreboard, 82
* a year's supply of Power Bars, 129
* an autograph of his or her favorite sports star, 155
* a gift certificate to an indoor rock climbing wall, 22
* outdoor games (badminton, smashball, croquet, or volley-ball), 110

Someone You Barely Know

* a calendar of special days, 3
* blank books and journals, 26
* Hammond New Century World Atlas, 22
* beeswax candles, 111
* paperwhite narcissus bulbs, 13
* a gift basket from Balducci's, 57
* Pocket Survival Tool, 108
* a photo album, 23
* an olive wreath, 113
* flowers, 83

* the all-purpose thank-you basket, 168
* a silver Swiss Army knife, 172

Young at Heart
* Nerf and Koosh toys, 18
* Victorian mansion dollhouse, 20
* walkie-talkies, 19
* Magic 8-Ball, 109
* a yo-yo, 27
* Slinky, 27
* an Easy-Bake Oven, 27
* personalized game board, 88
* SnowShorts, 108
* a box of kids' toys, 27
* candy kaleidoscope, 105
* flying or glider lessons, 32
* a red gumball machine, 109
* a carnivorous plant, 16
* Erector sets, 105

The Practical Person
* a course in financial planning, 27
* a personal organizer, 61
* *The Stanley Complete Step-by-Step Book of Home Repair and Improvement* (Simon & Schuster), 61
* flannel sheets, 89
* a gift certificate for a cleaning service, 29
* Pocket Survival Tool, 108
* a tool chest, 41
* a snow shovel, 59
* *The New York Public Library Desk Reference* (Macmillan), 123
* a stormproof umbrella, 47
* an emergency preparedness kit, 61

For Someone Who Has Everything
* a paint-your-own ceramic piece, 21
* personalized stationery, 42
* Menu of the Month, 44
* a gift basket from Balducci's, 57
* Clambakes-to-Go, 58
* embroidered cashmere pillow shams, 89
* an electrically heated towel rack, 112
* a donation in his name to Habitat for Humanity, 114

The Outdoors Lover
* wind chimes, 59
* binoculars, 27
* field guides, 27
* a new fishing pole, 53
* a rain gauge and thermometer, 128
* a hammock, 48
* a backpack, 121
* a picnic basket, 43
* a star named in his honor, 93
* outdoor games (badminton, smashball, croquet, or volleyball), 110
* Swiss Army compass, 108
* Pocket Survival Tool, 108
* membership to the Fly of the Month Club, 118
* two weeks with Outward Bound, 127

The Couch Potato
* cordless phone, 23
* universal remote control, 152
* breakfast in bed, 26
* a magazine subscription, 26
* personalized game board, 88
* a Polarfleece wrap, 112
* a fireside blanket, 112
* Foot Duvet, 112
* a hammock, 48

* popcorn, seasonings, and a bowl, 62
* a monogrammed cold drink holder, 149
* a sampling of micro-brewery beers, 62

The Gourmet

* Menu of the Month, 44
* a bottle of wine from the year he was born, 28
* a Laguiole knife from France, 53
* a gift basket from Balducci's, 57
* jams, mustards, oil, and vinegar from Stonewall Kitchens, 57
* a heart-shaped cutting board, 83
* a membership to the Wine of the Month Club, 117
* mulling spices, 113
* Clambakes-to-Go, 58
* cooking classes, 129
* a hand-crank ice cream maker, 110
* copper cooking accessories, 52

The Dieter

* a basket from Manhattan Fruitier, 58
* Heart Healthy gift basket, 90
* a jump rope, 18
* a juicer, 115
* a cookbook, 115
* a fanny pack with water bottle, 115
* membership to the Harry & David Fruit of the Month Club, 116
* Gourmet Greens & Vegetable Sampler, 167
* a teapot with tea, 47

For One Who Loves the Finer Things

* willow picnic hamper, 43
* silver-plated watering can, 43
* goatskin photo album, 43
* 1 kilo of Beluga caviar, 87
* a membership to the Wine-of-the-Month Club, 117
* a cashmere and silk robe, 90
* Flower ice cream by mail, 84

* embroidered cashmere pillow shams, 89
* calfskin jewelry case, 92
* membership to the Monthly Cigar Club, 117
* a joyride in a MiG-29 jet, 148

The Great Romantic
* heart-shaped Limoges box, 35
* a book of love poems, 79
* ballroom dancing lessons, 37
* silk or satin sheets, 89
* a gift for the five senses, 93
* chocolate love letters, 89
* a star named in her honor, 93
* *How to Write Love Letters* (Shooting Star Press), 80
* breakfast in bed, 26
* The Romance Gift Box, 85

The Homebound
* cordless phone, 23
* Personal Book Club, 116
* a magazine subscription, 29
* a subscription to an internet service provider, 31
* coupons to do the grocery shopping, 138
* Menu of the Month, 44
* flowering plant of the month, 117
* An emergency preparedness kit, 61
* an electrically heated towel rack, 112
* an aromatherapy candle, 95
* The Foot Duvet, 112
* a down comforter, 112
* a Polarfleece wrap, 112
* a bed desk, 135
* a colorful bulletin board, 136
* fragrant potpourri, 140

A New Grandparent

* a blank cassette to record a bedtime story for baby, 15
* a videotape of the new one, 68
* *Legacy: A Step-by-Step Guide to Writing a Personal History* (Swallow Press), 30
* *Little Things Mean a Lot: Creating Happy Memories with Your Grandchildren* (Crown Publishing), 154
* *Grandmother's Treasures* (Crown Publishing), 155
* a custom calendar with photos of the grandkids, 154
* made-to-size handprint cookie cutters, 155
* a necklace with tiny sterling silver ring set with baby's birthstone, 148
* a journal to record family memories, 26
* gift certificate for a photo shoot, 68
* a locket for the new grandma, 75
* a mini-photo album for proud grandpa, 154

The Computer Nut

* a laptop-toting computer gargoyle, 163
* a leather mouse pad, 124
* miniature keyboard vacuum cleaner, 163
* a milk chocolate P.C., 163
* a subscription to an online internet service provider, 31
* E-greetings, 163
* a gift certificate to a local electronic store, 22

The Vegetarian

* Mammarella's pasta sauce, 44
* Menu of the Month, 44
* a basket from Manhattan Fruitier, 58
* heart-shaped pasta, 83
* Heart Healthy gift basket, 90
* membership to the Harry & David Fruit of the Month Club, 116
* a juicer, 115
* Gourmet Greens & Vegetable Sampler with Organic Flowers, 167

The Do-It-Yourselfer

* *The Pocket Idiot's Guide to Trouble-Free Home Repair* (Macmillan General Reference), 61
* Pocket Survival Tool, 108
* brew-your-own rootbeer kit, 109
* *The Stanley Complete Step-by-Step Book of Home Repair and Improvement* (Simon & Schuster), 61
* *The Pocket Ref* (Sequoia Publishing), 149
* A gift certificate to a local hardware store, 63

The Bibliophile or Writer

* Waterman and Mont Blanc pens, 26
* Firenze journal, 26
* a bed desk, 135
* *In Their Own Voices: A Century of Recorded Poetry* (Rhino Records), 80
* membership to the Personal Book Club, 116
* membership to the Crossword Club, 118
* antiquarian signed first editions, 152
* a traveler's writing chest, 47
* a gilt-edged, moroccan-bound first edition of *The Great Gatsby*, 152
* scented inks from France, 80

The Workaholic

* a red gumball machine for her desk, 109
* a monogrammed calfskin envelope for business cards, 161
* monogrammed memo pads, 124
* a leather mouse pad, 124
* a beautiful vase, 159
* *How to Draw a Radish and Other Fun Things to Do at Work* (Chronicle Books), 161
* *Shakespeare's Insults for the Office* (Clarkson Potter), 161
* a gift certificate for an in-office massage therapist, 164
* a plug-in coffee warmer, 163
* a subscription to *The Wall Street Journal*, 124

The Socially Conscious Person
* gift basket from the Body Shop, 23
* plant half an acre of soybeans in his name to feed the hungry in Bangladesh, 114
* a donation in her name to the American Heart Association, 90
* plant a tree in his name, 52
* Until They Find a Cure Bracelet benefiting AIDS research, 114
* adopt a whale, 114
* a membership to a local public radio station, 114

For One Who Loves Wheels
* a model car or bike from his year of birth, 23
* race car driving classes, 32
* detail her car inside and out, 153
* Matchbox cars, 23
* Roadside Safety Kit, 127
* a Harley-Davidson business card case, 152
* Porsche Boxster, 151
* a grooming kit for the car or bike, 152
* a sterling silver key ring, 127
* rent him a Ferrari for the day, 153

Service People (your doorman, postal worker, cleaning person, etc.)
* a gift certificate to an electronics store, 22
* the all-purpose Thank You basket, 168
* warm and fuzzy Polarfleece gloves, 112
* homemade cookies, 86
* The Sunshine Sampler from Starbucks, 136
* a manicure and pedicure gift certificate, 75

The Business Traveler

* Send a song to his hotel, 7
* Audio Editions, 30
* a globe, 25
* Foot Duvet, 112
* Golf camp, 131
* tin of traveler's tea, 47
* a good book, 46
* Braun travel alarm clock, 47
* engraved brass luggage tags, 47
* Ready-to-Go Travel Kit, 47
* a travel pillow, 47

The Executive

* a sterling silver Swiss Army Knife, 172
* rent a Ferrari, 153
* Personal Book Club, 116
* travel umbrella, 47
* Membership to Wine-of-the-Month Club, 117
* Race car driving lessons, 32
* Life magazine from the week of her birth, 27
* Caran d'Ache pen, 165
* a sterling silver yo-yo, 159
* red calf leather and brass desk set, 159
* theater tickets, 44

The Discerning Teen

* money!, 24
* a private telephone line, 23
* single-use, wide-angle camera, 23
* chocolate chip cookies, 24
* gift certificate to her favorite clothing store, 22
* gift certificate to Tower Records or Virgin MegaStore, 24
* a facial, 75
* Walkman and blank tapes, 106
* cash earmarked for snowboarding trip, 24
* membership to Boxer of the Month Club, 116

* Until There's a Cure AIDS bracelet, 114
* a car, 123
* Paul Sloane's lateral thinking books, 105

Tried-and-True Children's Gifts
* sidewalk chalk, 102
* a spinning top, 105
* Legos, 105
* children's classic books, 104
* a red tricycle or bicycle, 108
* matchbox cars, 23
* a Slinky, 27
* a Frisbee, 17
* art supplies, 17
* Chimalong, 108
* easel with chalkboard and paint tray, 17
* tape recorder, 15
* rocking chair, 11

Appendix B

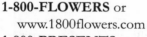

Sources

1-800-FLOWERS or
  www.1800flowers.com
1-800-PRESENTS or
  www.1800present.com.
1-800-SAUCES-1
4 My Love at www.4mylove.com
911 Gifts at www.911gifts.com
A Child's Dream, 800-359-2906 or
  www.home.earthlink.net/~todream/
A. G. A. Correa & Son, 800-341-0788 or www.agacorrea.com
Aardvark Pets, www.aardvarkpet.com
Ad Hoc Softwares, 212-925-2652
Adventures in Cassettes, 800-328-0108 or www.aic-radio.com
Alfred Dunhill, 800-860-8362
Alternative Gifts International, 800-842-2243 or www.altgifts.org
Amazon.com, www.amazon.com
American Girl Catalog, 800-845-0005 or www.americangirl.com
American Heart Association, 800-AHA-USA1 or www.amhrt.org
American Science & Surplus, 847-982-0870 or www.sciplus.com
Animal Town, 800-445-8642 or www.animaltown.com

Anyone's Game, 800-448-5431

Art Institute of Chicago, 800-621-9337 or www.artic.edu

Asprey, 212-688-1811

Audio Editions, 800-231-4261 or www.audioeditions.com

Audubon, 800-274-4201

Baccarat, 800-777-0100

Balducci's, 800-BALDUCCI or www.balducci.com

Barnes & Noble, www.barnesandnoble.com

Barneys, 212-826-8900 or www.netcity.com/barneysny.html

Bath-of-the-Month Club, 800-406-BATH or www.mudbath.com

Bergdorf Goodman, 800-218-4918

Bits & Pieces, 800-JIGSAWS or www.bits&pieces.com

Blankees, 888-BLANKEE or www.blankees.com

Bloomingdale's by Mail, 800-777-0000 or
  www.bloomingdalesbymail.com

Body Shop, 800-BODYSHOP or www.the-body-shop.com

Book Passage, fax: 415-924-3838
  or e-mail: messages@bookpassage.com

Borders Books and Music, www.borders.com

Bowl Mill, 802-824-6219

Brookstone, 800-926-7000 or www.brookstoneonline.com

Buckeye Beans & Herbs, 800-449-2121
  or www.buckeyeranch.com

Business Week, 800-635-1200

By the Vine, 888-298-4384 or www.bythevine.com

Calyx and Corolla, 800-800-7788 or www.calyxandcorolla.com

Catholic Supply of St. Louis, 800-325-9026
  or www.catholicsupply.com

Caviarteria, 800-4-CAVIAR or www.caviarteria.com

Celebration Fantastic, 800-CELEBRATE

Celestial Seasonings, 800-2000-TEA

Chambers, 800-334-9790

Chelsea Market Baskets, 888-727-7887
  or www.chelseamarketbaskets.com

Chinaberry Books, 800-776-2242

Christofle, 800-683-4619 or www.christof.com

Cigar Aficionado, 800-992-2442 or www.cigaraficionado.com

Clambakes-to-Go, 800-423-4038 or www.netplaza.com/clambake
Classics of Golf, 800-339-0745 or www.classicsofgolf.com
Colorado Pen Company, 800-766-PENS or www.coloradopen.com
Community Playthings, 800-777-4244
Company Store, 800-285-3696 or www.thecompanystore.com
Cookie Cutters by Karen, 888-476-4525
Crate and Barrel Bridal Registry, 800-967-6696
Crate and Barrel Catalog, 800-323-5461
Create-a-Book, 800-598-1044 or www.hefty.com
Crossword Club, 800-874-8100
Custom Specialtees, 415-551-9700
Daily 2-3-5, 212-334-9728
Dandelion, 888-548-1968
Daniel Smith, 800-426-6740
Dean & Deluca, 800-221-7714 or www.dean-deluca.com
Diamond Organics, 888-ORGANIC or www.diamondorganics.com
Disney Catalog, 800-237-5751 or www.disneystore.com
Duracell Holiday Toy Shopping Hot Line, 800-BEST TOYS
Dutch Gardens, 800-818-3861 www.dutchgardens.nl
E.A.T., 212-772-0022
Eastern Mountain Sports, 888-463-6367 or www.emsonline.com
Echo Wilderness Company, 800-652-ECHO, or
   www.echotrips.com
Eddie Bauer, 800-426-8020 or www.eddiebauer.com
Elderhostel, 617-426-8056 or www.elderhostel.org
European Travel & Life, 800-627-7660
Eurorail Pass, 800-722-7151
Eximious, 800-221-9464
Exposures, 800-222-4947 or www.mileskimball.com
Felissimo, 800-565-6785 or www.felissimo.com
Fillamento, 415-931-2224
Fire Robin Puppets, 800-235-5013
Fishing Enthusiast, 800-597-0634, or www.planetfish.pair.com
Flax, 800-547-7778 or www.flaxart.com
Fly with Us, 800-335-9538
Flying Noodle, 800-566-0599 or www.flyingnoodle.com
For Counsel, 800-637-0098 or www.forcounsel.com

Fortune, 800-621-8000 or www.fortune.com

Fortunoff's, 800-FORTUNOFF or www.fortunoff.com

Fountain Pen Hospital, 212-964-0580 or
   www.fountainpenhospital.com

Frontgate, 800-626-6488 or www.frontgate.com

Gap Kids or Baby Gap, 800-333-7899 or www.gap.com

Garden Design, 800-234-5118

Garden Escape, www.2garden.com

Gardener, 510-548-4545

Garnet Hill, 800-622-6216

Godiva Chocolatier, 800-9-GODIVA or www.godiva.com

Golf Digest, 800-PAR-GOLF

Good Vibrations, 800-289-8423 or www.goodvibes.com

Greet Street, www.greetst.com

H & H Bagels, 800-NY-BAGELS

Habitat for Humanity, 800-334-3308 or www.habitat.org

Hammacher Schlemmer, 800-543-3366 or www.hammacher.com

Hand in Hand, 800-872-9745

Hanna Anderson, 800-222-0544 or www.hannanderson.com

Harley-Davidson, 800-LUV-2-RIDE or www.harley-davidson.com.

Harmony, 800-456-1177

Harry & David, 800-842-6111, or www.harryanddavid.com

Hearthsong, 800-325-2502

Heirloom Old Garden Roses, 503-538-1576

Herrington, 800-903-2878

Hershey's, 800-454-7737 or www.hersheys.com

Highlights, 800-253-8688

Hogshead Beer Sellers, 800-795-BEER or www.hogshead.com

Hold Everything, 800-421-2264

IKEA, 800-434-4532 or www.ikea.com

Illuminations, 800-CANDLES or www.1800candles.com

International Herald Tribune, 800-882-2884 or www.iht.com

International Star Registry, 800-282-3333 or www.starregistry.com

International Wildlife Coalition, 508-548-8328 or www.icw.org

Iron Works Barbecue, 800-669-3602 or
   www.citysearch.com\aus\ironworksbbq

J. Crew, 800-562-0258 or www.jcrew.com

J. Peterman, 800-231-7341 or www.jpeterman.com

J. W. Bentley, 510-820-6648

Jewish National Fund, 212-879-9300

Kate's Paperie, 800-809-9880

L. L. Bean, 800-221-4221 or www.llbean.com

La Maison du Chocolat, 212-744-7117

Lamby Nursery Collection, 800-669-0527

Langenbach, 800-362-1991

Le Cordon Bleu, 800-457-CHEF or www.cordonbleu.net

Leonidas, 212-980-2608 or www.leonidas.com

Levenger, 800-544-0880 or www.levenger.com

Lighter Side, 941-747-2356

Lillian Vernon, 800-285-5555 or www.lillianvernon.com

Lilliput Motor Company, Ltd., 800-TIN-TOYS

Little Pilgrims Catalog, 888-475-4767

Logee's Greenhouses, 888-330-8038 or www.logees.com

Manhattan Fruitier, 800-841-5718 or www.nystyle.com/manfruit

Metropolitan Museum of Art, 800-662-3397 or
    www.metmuseum.org

Mill Valley Market Wine Shop, 800-699-4634

Mind's Eye, 800-949-3333 or www.netplaza.com/mindseye

MindWare, 800-999-0398

Miss Grace Lemon Cake Company, 800-FOR-CAKE

Money, 800-633-9970 or www.pathfinder.com/money

Monthly Cigar Club, 800-89-TASTE

Mrs. Field's, 800-344-CHIP or www.mrsfields.com

Muffin of the Month Club, 800-742-2403

Museum of Jewelry, 800-835-2700
    or www.museumofjewelry.com

Museum of Modern Art, 800-793-3167 or www.moma.org

Museum of Natural History Adventure Travel Department,
    800-462-8687

National Archives, 800-234-8861 or www.nara.gov

National Wildlife Federation, 800-588-1650

Natural Wonders, 800-2WONDERS

Nature Company, 800-227-1114 or www.natureco.com

New Penny Farm, 800-827-7551 or
www.mainerec.com/newpen.html
New York Times, 800-631-2580 or www.nytimes.com
Newsweek, 800-631-1040
Niebaum-Coppola Estate Winery, 707-968-1100
Norm Thompson, 800-547-1160 or www.normthompson.com
Original Time Capsule Company, 800-729-8463 or
www.timecap.com
Orvis, 800-541-3541 or www.orvis.com
Out of a Flower, Inc., 800-743-4696
Outward Bound, 800-243-8520 or www.outwardbound.org
Overseas Adventure Travel, 800-353-6262
Papyrus, 800-872-7978 or www.papyrus-spores.com
Patagonia, 800-638-6464 or www.patagonia.com
Peet's Coffee, 800-999-2132 or www.peets.com
Petrossian, 212-245-0303
Piece of Cake, 800-922-5390
Pinwheels, 425-488-0949
Pottery Barn, 800-922-5507
Pratesi, 800-332-6925 or www.pratesi.com
Renaissance Spa Treatments, 800-406-BATH or
www.mudbath.com
Resource Renewal Institute, 415-928-3774 or www.rri.org
Restoration Hardware, 800-762-1005 or
www.restorationhardware.com
Richart Design and Chocolate, 800-RICHART
San Francisco Music Box Company, 800-227-2190
Sandler's Gift Baskets, 800-75-FRUIT
Sarabeth's, 800-PRESERVE or www.sarabeth.com
Seeds of Change, 888-762-7333 or www.seedsofchange.com
Self-Care, 800-345-3371 or selfcare.com
SEND-A-SONG, 800-736-3276
SEVA Foundation, 800-223-7382 or www.seva.org
Sharper Image, 800-344-4444 or www.sharperimage.com
Signals, 800-669-9696
Smith & Hawken, 800-776-3336 or www.smith-hawken.com

Smithsonian, 800-766-2149
Snowboarding, 888-TWS-MAGS
Sonoma Antique Apples, 707-433-6420 or www.applenursery.com
Source for Everything Jewish, 800-426-2567 or
   www.jewishsource.com
Spice of the Month Club, 888-8-SPICES
The Sports Authority, 888-LOOK-4-TSA or
   www.sportsauthority.com
Sports Illustrated for Kids, 800-633-8628 or www.sikids.com
Starbucks, 800-STARBUC
Star Magic, www.starmagic.com
Stone Soup, 800-447-4569 or www.stonesoup.com
Stonewall Kitchens, 800-207-JAMS or www.stonewallkitchen.com
Summer House, 415-383-6695
Sunset, 800-777-0177
Supergram, 800-3-BANNER or www.supergram.com
Sur La Table, 800-243-0852
Susan G. Komen Breast Cancer Foundation, 972-867-5667
Tea Club, 800-FULL-LEAF
Teuscher Chocolates of Switzerland, 800-554-0924 or
   www.teuscherchocolate.com
Tiffany's, 800-526-0649
Time, 800-541-1000
Title Nine Sports, 510-655-5999 or www.title9sports.com
Tower Records, 800-648-4844 or www.towerrecords.com
Training Camp, 800-ATHLETE or www.thetrainingcamp.com
Travel & Leisure, 800-888-8728 or www.travelandleisure.com
Travelsmith, 800-995-7010 or www.travelsmith.com
U. S. Postal Service, 888-STAMP FUN or www.stampsonline.com
Victoria's Secret, 800-888-1500
Video Yesteryear, 800-243-0987
Virtual Vineyard, 800-289-1275 or www.virtualvineyard.com
Wall Street Journal, 800-568-7625 or www.info.wsj.com
Western Union, 800-325-6000
Whispering Pines, 800-836-4662
White Flower Farm, 800-503-9624 or www.whiteflowerfarm.com

White House Greetings Office, fax 202-395-1232
Whole Foods Markets, www.wholefoods.com
Williams-Sonoma, 800-541-2233 or www.williams-sonoma.com
Wind and Weather, 800-922-9463
Wireless, 800-669-9999 or www.giftcatalog.com
Wolfman Gold & Good Company, 212-431-1888
Womanswork, 800-536-2305
Wood Classics, 914-255-7871

A Year of Holidays

Listed below are some of the U.S. holidays you may want to remember in your perpetual calendar. This list is by no means exhaustive—you will want to add your own personal favorites, along with all of the birthdays and anniversaries you observe. Use the space following to note dates, and jot down sizes, preferences, and interests of your gift recipients.

January 1	New Year's Day
February 14	Valentine's Day
March 17	St. Patrick's Day
March 20	Vernal Equinox
March or April	Easter Sunday
April 1	April Fool's Day
April 22	Earth Day
Fourth Wednesday in April	Secretary's Day
Last Friday in April	Arbor Day
May 1	May Day

May 6	Nurses' Day
Second Sunday in May	Mother's Day
Last Monday in May	Memorial Day
Third Sunday in June	Father's Day
June 21	Summer Solstice
July 4	Independence Day
Fourth Sunday in July	Parents' Day
First Sunday in August	Friendship Day
First Monday in September	Labor Day
Sunday after Labor Day	Grandparents' Day
September 23	Autumnal Equinox
Second Sunday in October	Children's Day
October 16	Boss Day
Third Saturday in October	Sweetest Day
October 31	Halloween
November 11	Veterans Day
Fourth Thursday in November	Thanksgiving
November or December	First Day of Hanukkah
December 22	Winter Solstice
December 25	Christmas
December 26	First Day of Kwanzaa

JANUARY

1 ....
2 ....
3 ....
4 ....
5 ....
6 ....
7 ....
8 ....
9 ....
10 ....
11 ....
12 ....
13 ....
14 ....
15 ....
16 ....
17 ....
18 ....
19 ....
20 ....
21 ....
22 ....
23 ....
24 ....
25 ....
26 ....
27 ....
28 ....
29 ....
30 ....
31 ....

FEBRUARY

1
2
3
4
5
6
7
8
9
10
11
12
13
14
15
16
17
18
19
20
21
22
23
24
25
26
27
28
29

MARCH

1 ....
2 ....
3 ....
4 ....
5 ....
6 ....
7 ....
8 ....
9 ....
10 ....
11 ....
12 ....
13 ....
14 ....
15 ....
16 ....
17 ....
18 ....
19 ....
20 ....
21 ....
22 ....
23 ....
24 ....
25 ....
26 ....
27 ....
28 ....
29 ....
30 ....
31 ....

APRIL

1
2
3
4
5
6
7
8
9
10
11
12
13
14
15
16
17
18
19
20
21
22
23
24
25
26
27
28
29
30

MAY

1
2
3
4
5
6
7
8
9
10
11
12
13
14
15
16
17
18
19
20
21
22
23
24
25
26
27
28
29
30
31

JUNE

1
2
3
4
5
6
7
8
9
10
11
12
13
14
15
16
17
18
19
20
21
22
23
24
25
26
27
28
29
30

JULY

1
2
3
4
5
6
7
8
9
10
11
12
13
14
15
16
17
18
19
20
21
22
23
24
25
26
27
28
29
30
31

AUGUST

1 ....
2 ....
3 ....
4 ....
5 ....
6 ....
7 ....
8 ....
9 ....
10 ....
11 ....
12 ....
13 ....
14 ....
15 ....
16 ....
17 ....
18 ....
19 ....
20 ....
21 ....
22 ....
23 ....
24 ....
25 ....
26 ....
27 ....
28 ....
29 ....
30 ....
31 ....

SEPTEMBER

1
2
3
4
5
6
7
8
9
10
11
12
13
14
15
16
17
18
19
20
21
22
23
24
25
26
27
28
29
30

OCTOBER

1 ....
2 ....
3 ....
4 ....
5 ....
6 ....
7 ....
8 ....
9 ....
10 ....
11 ....
12 ....
13 ....
14 ....
15 ....
16 ....
17 ....
18 ....
19 ....
20 ....
21 ....
22 ....
23 ....
24 ....
25 ....
26 ....
27 ....
28 ....
29 ....
30 ....
31 ....

NOVEMBER

1
2
3
4
5
6
7
8
9
10
11
12
13
14
15
16
17
18
19
20
21
22
23
24
25
26
27
28
29
30

DECEMBER

1 ....
2 ....
3 ....
4 ....
5 ....
6 ....
7 ....
8 ....
9 ....
10 ....
11 ....
12 ....
13 ....
14 ....
15 ....
16 ....
17 ....
18 ....
19 ....
20 ....
21 ....
22 ....
23 ....
24 ....
25 ....
26 ....
27 ....
28 ....
29 ....
30 ....
31 ....

About the Author

Chiquita Woodard has spent the past fifteen years as a professional buyer, roaming the globe in search of great gifts. She served as director of merchandising for Smith & Hawken for ten years and was a buyer for The Nature Company. She has worked on special projects for companies including Felissimo and Ballard Design, as well as merchandising a catalogue for Cher. She is currently the buyer for Francis Ford Coppola's winery and was recently the Gift Expert for America OnLine, where she helped millions of subscribers solve their gift dilemmas. Ms. Woodard lives in Northern California with her husband and their three sons.

Index